Up Aloft with Old Harry

Bought at the
Ocean Bookshop

QUEEN ELIZABETH 2

CUNARD

Other titles by Des Sleightholme

Anchor's Aweigh
ISBN 0-7136-4812-0
In his usual hilarious tongue-in-cheek manner, Des Sleightholme introduces the newcomer to the joys of cruising, explaining how to go about choosing a boat, what is likely to happen on your first time out, coping with tides, knots, as well as etiquette and how to behave in marinas. Read it and you'll curl up!

Off Watch with Old Harry
ISBN 0-7136-4828-7
The 'joys' of antifouling, the bloody-mindedness of marine engines, the dubious pleasure of sailing on a spring tide, launchings and novice crew are just some of the subjects aired by Old Harry.

Old Harry's Dog Watch
ISBN 0-7136-4508-3
Perceptive, amusing and presented in his inimitable style, Des takes us through further nautical hair-raising experiences. An ideal bunkside read.

Up Aloft with Old Harry

DES SLEIGHTHOLME

ADLARD COLES NAUTICAL
London

First published 1999 by Adlard Coles Nautical
an imprint of A & C Black (Publishers) Ltd
35 Bedford Row, London WC1R 4JH

ISBN 0–7136–5040–0

A CIP catalogue record for this book is available from
the British Library

Typeset in 10/13pt Concorde

Printed and bound in Great Britain
by J W Arrowsmith Ltd, Bristol.

Note: Seven of the pieces in this book are reprinted with
the kind permission of *Yachting Monthly*

Contents

Preface

The potholer who accidentally enters the sewer system and whose uneasy progress can be monitored thereafter by watching the manholes as they pop up is closely similar to the progress of Old Harry through the following pages. His appearances and abrupt disappearances are a marble in the boot of a smooth flow of narrative, and the reader may find it unsettling.

The reader will be a damn sight less unsettled than we who knew the *real* Old Harry some forty years ago. He was an uneasy companion. 'Look,' he said one day in his shed, 'you won't find the ten-bore shotgun anywhere. Look where you will,' he invited generously, 'you won't find a gun with a smoother trigger action than this!'

To demonstrate his claim he pressed it. And blew the window straight out of the wall.

I am told by admirers that these little books are well received; they will cure wobbly tables and they are the right format to take a pint mug of tea and a jam butty. They make a welcome low-budget, thank-you-for-having-me gift (and you won't be going back *there* again), and one reader tells me that they are ideal for leaving in the loo, doubtless suspended from a string through one corner and sanitised for your protection.

Another reader was less than reassuring. He tapped the book with a forefinger. 'The wife's father went like 'im,' he said unsmilingly, 'in the end!'

J D Sleightholme

'So round the headland, bear away and it's all downhill thereafter Olaf!'

Up the Pole

Before the bosun's chair is tried
The galley skylight open wide
Should you then fall from aloft
With luck you'll land on something soft
And suffer not the slightest graze,
In the spaghetti bolognaze.

Modern mast-scaling owes little to your mountaineer, whacking in pitons and turning the mast into a piccolo. Still less does it owe to the sterner skills of Marine Commandos, blacked-up and abseiling straight down the forehatch where Norman is applying the tincture twice daily or as instructed by his physician. It owes more perhaps to the world of showbiz and the human cannonball, or maybe some mature Christmas Tree Fairy rising from splintered foliage.

The prospect of being hauled up a mast seems to attract muffins the way a sewage treatment works attracts novice hang-gliders, but the decision as to whom to send aloft is complex. Father, source of all knowledge, master of all maritime skills, is the obvious choice but he is also the heaviest, whereas Percy, being the lightest body aboard, seems the logical alternative. He will be about as much use up there as a stuffed cuckoo. His arrival at the masthead is celebrated by a rain of tools, small change and vital components. Why send him then, we may ask?

1

'Personally I don't see much point,' comments Father. He pauses to study the quivering marline spike buried several inches in the deck between his feet.

The performance involved in sending the Master aloft is productive of the shuddering sigh and the rolling eye. He begins by scorning the bosun's chair altogether, which nobody dreamed of using in his day. He proceeds to demonstrate – grunting, heaving and bicycling his way aloft to hook his chin over the crosstrees, there to lodge panting and scarlet-visaged, unable to gain another inch of altitude. 'That's... the general... idea,' he sobs before sliding down again with ignomiey.

Not even the provision of mast steps or ratlines – indeed *especially* with these aids – is he encouraged to go aloft. The Lady-wife is adamant. 'Not at your age and not wearing *those* shorts!' she proclaims.

The amount of actual work which can be carried out up there is limited. There is the routine spring check-up, which is supposed to reveal such potential disasters as stress cracks and the like. 'Oh, good,' people say, relieved. 'It's been *looked* at,' implying some rare mystical force at work. Maintenance is limited to a laying on of hands, a myth akin to the Black Shuck. Most such examiners wouldn't know a stress crack from a buttered scone.

Attention to the masthead collection of electronic gizmos and whirligigs is everybody's dread. The shackle on the bosun's chair is two blocks against the sheave, preventing further ascent and putting the task to be done on the level of your upper lip and out of focus. It is like kneeling at the breakfast table and tackling your boiled egg from the bottom upwards.

The vital tool will have been omitted from the cornucopia contained in the bucket. The missing tool can be sent aloft on a spare halyard though. Can't it?

Gentle reader who has been there, done it and got the T-shirt can be forgiven a mirthless laugh, for he knows that the halyard must always be an endless one. Otherwise there will come a moment when the weight of descending halyard becomes greater than that of the ascending tool, which thereafter hurtles aloft with ever-increasing acceleration. 'Wheeep!' cackles father, accepting delivery of a 10 inch fid.

Aboard your ocean racer in the marina there is never a shortage of volunteers to go aloft and be stared at. Once up there they carry on a booming (or falsetto – it depends on the type of chair being used) conversation with the deck. Casual listeners don't know what the hell they are talking about.

'Give me an inch on your bungling strop,' bellows some young Adonis in a headband, 'ease away your thrupping lead.' Father, on the other hand, while equally vocal, is more concerned with self-preservation.

'The turn, the turn, don't take the turn off!' he beseeches Hilda, as if hinting at some droll entertainment involving whitewash and a unicycle. The deck below him becomes about as lethal as a stroll past the OK Corral. Having made him fast with a multiplicity of figures-of-eight, she retires to the safety of the cockpit to wait. It is warmer down below on the settee. And she did have a late night.

Getting him aloft in the first place, aided only by a halyard winch the size of a potted-meat jar plus his gargantuan heaves, is the unhappy lot of many a wife, but it is still a mite better than going herself and being screamed at nonstop.

There are some ladies with an aptitude for this sort of thing, virtuosos on the hammer-drill and artistes with fid and spike, but Hilda, though a wizard with a net curtain, is not of their number.

For the ladies who do, in the end, succumb to bullying and find themselves treading thin air, the temptation to let drop the odd tool is overwhelming.

'No, no, no, on your left side... your LEFT,' he whines. Wistfully she visualises that hated bobble cap sprouting a rat-tail file. 'And while you are up there', he howls, 'my blocks need seizing and perhaps you'd like to give my antennae a good waggle.' Oh she would, she really would.

One of the most common emergencies calling for a trip aloft is the loss of a halyard end up the mast while sailing.

'I like to give beginners a chance to show what they can do,' states Father generously, watching from the cockpit as a couple of real cloth-eared dumbos set about lowering a sail. His benign smile becomes a death's-head rictus. 'No, no, make it faaa...!' he shrieks belatedly as the tail goes dancing aloft like some will-o'-the-wisp. There follows a sort of boathook ballet, each crew member in turn convinced that he or she has the necessary skill, swiping and thrusting at the soaring, leaping rope's end. Nobody wins.

'*I'll* have to go... up there,' says the Master, features working convulsively. Harnessed like Old Dobbin he is cranked a full 5 ft above the boom to effect a recovery, swooping around like some monstrous spider.

Just as overhead wires attract hordes of migrant starlings, so ratlines, which offer easy access to the crosstrees, lure aloft the daysail novice while friends below take innumerable photos up their trouser legs. Old Harry's converted pollocker is rarely seen without these roosting figures, driven aloft usefully armed with slush-pot and other beneficial nostrums. Aboard his state-of-the-art bosun's chair, which has holes to accommodate a variety of life-threatening tools, he invites disaster like a Welsh dresser on a roof rack. Maintenance aloft is carried out on an almost daily basis, due to the depredations of rust, rot and mildew, which sounds like a firm of solicitors – and don't ever let that Mildew man get near my briefs.

Slushing down the lower mast with mutton fat wins him the gratitude of bluebottles throughout the county. It also lubricates the neighbourhood to leeward and the pontoon in particular, where a lady in bursting jeans and a frontage like a tympanum can be seen running on the spot with a load of groceries. Worse is to come: varnishing the topmast.

Enlisting the aid of a passing troop of Boy Scouts to tail on the halyard, Old Harry goes soaring aloft like some renaissance martyr, paradise-bound and running late. It is not without its drama. Under the healthy impetus of enthusiastic young muscles he rockets skywards, whamming up against the truck.

'Avast heavin' come up all,' he warns.

Instantly the lads let go and commence swarming aloft, except for one beetle-wit whose outsize beret was resting on his

ears, rendering him incommunicado, and who therefore hangs on. There is a brief exchange of views between the descending Old Harry and the ascending child. 'Awwwwk!' they chorus.

Eventually, and using the gantline hitch (which sounds like some scrofulous tropical skin complaint), he begins a controlled descent in a series of heart-stopping plunges, varnishing lustily the while. The area to leeward is quickly cordoned off by the police using yellow tape. Residents in carpet slippers, with canaries and bare essentials, are shepherded to safety. A fine mist of best copal settles over the district. A dowager, whose bouffant hair job now has the texture of a brandy snap, scuttles past at speed. A man with a hairpiece like a tame wombat now anchored for all time pauses in flight. 'Lacquered?' he enquires. 'No,' she says, 'I'm just panting a bit hard.'

'Itch gumming gite gown ger goregatch!' complains a yachtsman with stiffening features.

Bystanders, unaware of the crisis, study the sky. A fine rain of quick dry looks set in for the day. 'They never forecast this!' complains one. 'Still the gardeners have been crying out for it,' he adds, hinting at sobbing horticulturists.

'Here, share my umbrella.' 'Oh, I think I'll stick to my anorak,' his companion predicts with disturbing precognition.

An increase of wind strength from Force 1 to 3 (whole twigs in motion) gingers Father into action.

A Handle in Front

A swing bridge ahead
And the wind has gone dead
We've an engine to deal with that.
The starter goes 'Whah!'
Which won't get us fah
Who let the battery go flat?

Any auxiliary with a cast-iron ball on top and a handle in front plus an assortment of brass bits wins the instant approval of traditionalists. If the starting procedure leaves an owner with lolling tongue and sobbing for breath it is awarded the appellation of Grand Old Engine. It will have a flywheel that would suit a steam roller and it will be innocent of anything vaguely resembling a gearbox.

In the clangorous gloom of a galvanized iron shed a mildewed sail is pulled aside. The dust clears. 'By God that's a grand old engine!' chant admirers. They are willing to bet that given a drop of petrol and a couple of swings she'd be away. The further the better.

No prizes are offered for guessing the form of power plant lurking in Old Harry's reeking bilges. There it squats like some monstrous green toad poised over a quaggy drip-tray abrim with unspeakable mechanical filth. A well-burnished starting handle hints at years of harrowing labour.

Old Harry considers that ignition and feeling for top-dead-centre are needlessly dangerous pursuits. It is designed to start on the hot bulb principle – a method not to be confused with father juggling a hot and defunct lamp in the outside toilet. It involves a roaring blowlamp and a nerve-jangling wait, rewarded by a thumping, shuddering progress beneath by a canopy of smoke rings.

That old engine will rock and snuffle away by the hour. You could wind wool on that tail shaft; it rattles away like a scratching dog under a table. Once she's warm she'd run on bread and milk. Not for him the starter motor, batteries and the probing hydrometer. He gave up hydrometers the time he used one to syringe out an ear full of sump oil. His battery hasn't held a charge since.

If an engine won't start he has an infallible solution. His crew always includes a novice possessed of a healthy desire to learn, plus a vast and natural stupidity. In a calm, with the plugs out and priming cocks open, the most moribund of engines can be cranked around by a panting tyro to the tune of a couple of knots.

You've got to be able to get at an engine. Builders working to quantity production methods install the engine prior to adding the deck, which is like putting your wellies on before your Y-fronts. It makes maintenance a task for athletes and calls for the abdominal gyrations of a belly dancer. A yard engineer with a ruby in his navel is a disturbing spectacle.

You get the choice of either seeing what you are doing but being unable to reach it or reaching it blind and working by touch. It makes keyhole surgery look like riddling cinders.

There is no excuse for an owner not understanding the engine; excellent courses are available under the auspices of your District Council Adult Education Classes, which deal with every subject from aromatherapy and folk dancing to corn dollies and car maintenance (any of the foregoing likely to be more rewarding than the latter).

Car maintenance offers a course of twelve winter evenings and deals with such esoteric matters as changing a gearbox, replacing clutch plates, brake liners and fixing leaky hydraulics.

Armed with this rich store of knowledge, Dad goes home and adjusts the wing mirror. Lady-wife complains that the steering feels funny. She wishes he wouldn't fiddle about.

Diesel auxiliary manufacturers also offer day seminars for wide-eyed owners ambitious to do their own maintenance and cut out regular visits from the teeth-sucking yard engineer – who don't like the look of them big ends, God's honour he don't.

Seminars start and end with coffee/tea, biscuits and leaflets. Students are confronted by an oil-free engine on a stand, cut away to show its gaily painted innards and suggesting tremendous internal explosions best not thought about. It is like a cadaver at a medical college lecture eyed by ashen-faced students all swallowing hard. They learn about injectors and power strokes, returning home confident that in an emergency they could change an impeller and dip a sump.

The modern small marine diesel is a model of efficiency and total reliability. (Let us pause for a moment, heads bowed in an act of silent prayer.) The owner has little to do beyond maintaining a wholesome diet of fuel, oil, water and the occasional titbit of a new filter.

The novice however is haunted by the grim thought that some day the engine may need to be bled. A nightmare operation conjuring up visions of Count Dracula in opera hat and flapping black cloak sucking away at his sump with ghoulish gusto, to be vanquished only by brandished crucifix or sharpened stake.

Having never known the era of the petrol auxiliary, the marinised Morris, fumes in the bilge and a sniffing spouse alert to the imminent possibility of being rocketed skywards riding on the engine-box lid, he should count his blessings. He can munch his diesel-flavoured bacon butty and mop his brow with diesel-scented handkerchief with an easy mind.

Of all the petrol engines, it is the two-stroke (an uneasy recollection of corporal punishment and an atlas down your breeks) that has made the greatest impact upon the marine scene, bent more pulpits and dissolved more marriages. It is remembered by many with a shudder of revulsion and revered by zealots with deep-set feverish eyes.

Typically it will remain dead throughout a frenzy of jerking on cord or handle. Everybody aboard joins in with advice. Some favour the two pulls to suck in followed by a heroic jerk and a double rupture, others opt for more Machiavellian methods.

'The last time it went first pull was when the forehatch was open', offers Muriel. Father splutters, spreads helpless hands, rolls eyes heavenwards. Has anybody ever heard anything so absurd he demands to know. The hatch is opened. The bastard bellows into life.

Usually it resists all such occult influences. It ignores all jerks no matter how heroic. It scorns a fresh plug, sneers at it being toasted on the cooker, ignores having its points pencilled... Then, for no good reason at all, it explodes into life at full throttle, rattling every pot, pan and bottle. The burgee chatters in sympathy. It is like a dangerous wild beast, sedated by a veterinary dart, awakening suddenly during treatment to abrupt and violent life and all hell breaking loose.

'Well if you ask me...' says Muriel. Nobody did. 'You'd better get somebody who *knows* about engines.' It is as if engines were some sort of seedy marital secret involving private dicks pretending to read upside-down newspapers.

What she has in mind is his brother-in-law – him with the transit van and the full socket set. He is never without his full socket set. His honeymoon was a failure. She took her mother and he took his full socket set.

The ultimate danger for the owner of a hand-start petrol auxiliary is a brother-in-law with a full socket set who can't keep his greasy paws off it. 'I think you'll notice a difference,' he promises. 'I've advanced your ignition a bit.' He does not exaggerate. Advancing the ignition a bit is in much the same category as sticking a thistle under the tail of an ill-tempered unbroken stallion.

It would be better, muses Father, if we had a twin pole arrangement. They would be about as much use to him as a pair of stilts to a bandy-legged gardener. Father will hum-haw for an hour, staring up the mast as if in search of heavenly guidance. The burgee hangs limply, fishing smacks have bare steerage, and ashore small leaves are stirring. By heaven, he'll do it!

Mum, who doesn't give a tuppenny damn which sail is set, is intent only upon tanning her spare tyre on the foredeck, an occupation which will stripe her horizontally in red and white, and which, in buoyage terms, entitles mariners to pass her either to port or starboard.

This privilege is roughly abused as the forehatch bursts open and Father emerges, like some homely dung beetle with its noisome prize, dragging the spinnaker bag.

'Oh you're not going to start fooling around with that thing!' she snarls. The cost of spinnaker, poles and snuffer, she reflects sourly, is comparable to a holiday for two, somewhere hot.

There will then follow an hour of diligent activity with ropes and poles, during which time the lee guy will be given a turn round the guardrail, ensuring a regular treat in store should anything as foolhardy as a gybe be attempted. Tension mounts as the time to hoist and break out approaches.

Like some failed conjuring trick, a gaily coloured bundle jerks aloft. There are apoplectic howls as it brushes the cross-trees. 'Sheet-sheet-sheet! Guy-guy-guy!' screams Father, leaping around. The bundle just hangs there in loops and swags, like the parlour curtains. All it lacks is a pot plant.

Setting a spinnaker is a defiance of fate. Aladdin, having blown down the spout of his Wonderful Lamp, need hardly be surprised at the emergence of the Genie mopping its eye and vowing vengeance. After much jerking around at pole and sheet, the sail fills. All stand back in admiration. Photos are taken. Lunch is dismissed with a scornful wave of the hand. Half an hour later, and with upraised moistened forefinger to assess wind strength, Father decides that it must be handed. Smacks may not as yet be making for harbour and whole trees are not yet in motion, but one cannot be too careful.

'Let's show 'em how to do it,' he declares unwisely.

'A nice quick drop then!' he encourages, a condemned man instructing his executioner. To ensure total disaster, he puts Norman on the halyard and nominates Percy to the crucial task of letting fly and gathering in.

With these two flopheads involved it is tantamount to leaving a brimming bucket of whitewash in a day nursery. Percy furrows a Neanderthal brow. He dimly remembers that the last time he went sailing it was the red corner that had to be unclipped...

The advent of the spinnaker sock should have robbed the sail of all threat. But if the setting and lowering of spinnakers is vulnerable to the ham-fisted, the *bagging* of one down below while leaping to windward in the unrated, unbelievable and unthinkable cruiser-racer is still rich ground for ten-thumbed ineptitude.

The saloon is swathed in a colourful ballooning mass, like some vast meringue, in which two wan-faced workers swim desperately. They are stuffing it back in its bag along with a washing-up towel, a wet sock, two pairs of knickers and a cheese-and-tomato sandwich.

Later, as the windward mark is rounded, the sail will soar aloft in a symbolic wineglass shape, distributing largesse like a Maundy Ceremonial. Muriel, who won't-be-spoken-to-like-that, quits the tiller and flounces below.

For that doyen of gaff rig Old Harry, whose topsail sets like a rag rug over a clothesline, the carrying of what he terms 'fancy stuff' becomes an art form. The flying staysail, set in stops, bursts into shape at the tug of a sheet, showering those on deck with a bonanza of spiders and pipe dottle. His converted eel-wrangler, when laid alongside, becomes a place of pilgrimage for students of traditional sail. Antiquarians cluster on the quayside noting with approval that the owner still has his little iron bumpkin and that his dandywink is in working order. Two maiden ladies from Crewe, down for the ozone and potted shrimps, listen in mounting alarm.

'I'd love to watch him tripping his fid!' notes an onlooker, disturbingly.

For the owners of gaff-rigged yachts, the setting of topsails is *de rigueur*. Novices adopt this responsibility with dry mouth and pounding heart. Topsails go shimmying up and down masts inverted and sideways like targets at a funfair. An orgy of photography accompanies success. Prints will show an acreage of mainsail topped by a brown smear. Pictorially, it's in the same style as family snaps of auntie in her deckchair with gargantuan kneecaps and a miniature head.

'All hands to take in topsail!' he howls point-blank at Nance, as she appears on deck with tea and biscuits. He then makes the gross error of appointing as helmsman Percy, whose grasp of practical seamanship is limited to the bunny-hole-and-tree method of tying a bowline. Percy's finest hour has come.

Reliable hands have been stationed at halyard, sheet and downhaul ready for a quick drop.

'When I nod my head give me a quick shake,' instructs Father, revealing a sorry trust in human nature – Percy's in particular.

'Like this, Uncle?' says that idiot, wagging his great daft poll.

'NO, BOY,' thunders Father, 'Like this...' nodding with vigour.

A barbed wire fence could be fed into a combine harvester with less dire effect than what follows. Percy bangs the helm hard over. Jib and staysail go hard aback, and three reliable hands release their grips. Like some monster skylark, the topsail, tethered only by its sheet, which has taken a turn around the end of the gaff, wings aloft into that great azure bowl on beating pinions. The flogging mainsheet snares and triggers off the liferaft just as the coil slides overboard. With masterly ill-timing Percy hits the engine starter button. GLUMP! goes the engine, stopping dead.

Father is on his hands and knees thumping his head on the deck. 'I'm going to *kill* him!' he chuckles eerily. 'I'm going to KILL him!'

It's Alright if it's Boiled

They got their money's worth
In the next door berth
They filled her up like a tanker
While they remained-there
They filled every container
Until they sank-her.

Father guards his water supply like a she-wolf with her cubs. At breakfast his jaws lock on a slice of toast and he listens intently, counting the pump strokes coming from the loo. '...eight, nine..' He intones crummily, '... fourteen, fifteen. Who's in there?' he demands loudly.

'Ethel,' says Lady-wife, enunciating silently, while raising the cautionary finger. Auntie Ethel, like everybody else aboard, wishes she'd never come. She has passed an embarrassing night with the gurgles of the flexible tank under her bunk, a phenomenon which she cannot explain, but blames on the broad beans.

'She will have to be told!' Father thunders. 'The yacht is not on the mains,' he explains. 'Water is precious!'

'Then get some more, for God's sake!' hisses Lady-wife, hinting at some solemn and sacred ritual involving candles and choirboys.

Which is the point at which Father trots out his 'one-pint-wash' claim.

17

'I can get a perfectly good wash all over in one pint of water,' he flutes. His one-pint-wash has become a myth which haunts the ship like some naiad of the woodland pool.

At intervals, and with painful ostentation, he retires to the loo with pint mug, towel and toothbrush. There follows a series of bangs and thuds, snatches of song and gasps of satisfaction, hinting at either ten rounds with a welterweight or ecstasies beyond the ken of ordinary mortals.

The average family ashore uses water like a burst main and the toilet flush is clunking and clanking day-long like a busy shunting yard. Once afloat, though, a state of drought prevails. This arid existence is no penalty for the one-bath-a-fortnight man but, conversely, your daily dipper migrates from one marina ablution block to the next where he can be heard gasping under the shower. 'Ahhh!' he coos. 'Eeeek,' he trebles, as his 50p's-worth runs out and the permafrost hits him. It's made a new man of him. It is a pronouncement that does little to cheer his tight-lipped spouse in the ladies' shower next door. The old one was bad enough.

Morning ablutions on board are another matter. Men splash about like a hen in a puddle. You would think they were putting out a fire. With eyes screwed up tight, they gasp and spit, gargle and grope around amidst flying tooth-mugs and unshipped toilet roll, leaving the place in a dripping shambles.

Women, on the other hand, seem to have the ability to glide in as if they were on casters, unobserved, wraithlike and there to remain in total silence for the next two tides. The next thing an onlooker might notice is that the loo door is now ajar, the place is empty and there is a faint scent of lilac in the air. Sailing women also acquire the delicate art of silent pump manip-ulation, noiselessly drawing off vast quantities of water – unlike Auntie Ethel's sturdy clunkings.

The electric pump has altered all this, though, and Father, whose other favourite gripe is the state of his batteries, is torn between the conservation of current and the satisfaction of being able to monitor water flow aurally.

Wheeeeep goes the pump. Wheee... wheeeeeep. 'Listen,

listen!' he howls. He hammers on the loo door. 'A pint, a pint. That's all you need!' he sobs.

Listening to the pump becomes a sort of shipboard community activity.

Since the advent of yacht marinas, the topping up of tanks has become a simple operation. In the old days you could spot a cruising yachtsman by the anthropoidal length of his arms, a disability caused by carrying water containers while plodding homeward over the mud.

Your laughing fellow rover would head unerringly for the solitary farmhouse, distantly visible over the sea wall, whose solitary occupant had only just got his head down after a night's vigil over a sick heifer. He bangs on the door for a third time, adjusts his smirk and waits. It opens. The farmer is minus cap, teeth and humour. He stands there scratching and scowling.

'I wonder if I can be a nuisance?' falters our mariner.

'I'm dang sure you can mate!' says our husbandman, whacking the door shut.

Most town slipways have a tap nearby – the bequest of some Edwardian Elder, pictured by contemporary photographers buttoned up to the glottis and apparently emerging from a jungle of potted palms. However, should the ground nearby be a quagmire, an irregularity of some kind may be suspected. It may be one of the following:

1. The tap calls for the grip of a strangler to budge it. Then it suddenly yields and shoots out sideways to widdle down your leg.
2. It turns easily, but yields only a wandering trickle and the water can needs to be hand-held for five minutes. Tortured muscles quiver. A tic develops in left eyelid, which is misinterpreted by a passing nun.
3. Flow commences straight and true, water can is positioned, whereupon it switches to crop-sprayer mode.
4. Spring-loaded button. The effort of holding the can up and the button in causes tic to develop, etc. It is misinterpreted by a passing navvy in a yellow hat.

5. Vandalised (ie yobs have practised self-expression). 'Haw, haw, haw, mate, seefyer can bend the hiccoughing hiccougher haw, haw, haw!' It now resembles a fountain and lacks only stone cupids, etc.

Bacteria-wise, the marina hosepipe, which has been dipped in the dock and left to broil in the sun, would make a septic tank look like the Bonny Falls O'Divach, should one be foolhardy enough to make a comparison. The public analyst staring at the primitive life forms in our tank water reports it as lethal at twenty paces. It would have blasted the Borgias like salted slugs. Father is undismayed. 'It will be all right if it's boiled,' he defends stoutly.

Flavour is something else. Ask a wine connoisseur. He has most probably braved the neighbour's peapod with scarcely a whimper, but one sip of Father's tank water and he rears up like a striking cobra, clutches his throat and then expectorates with a violence that sets the bucket rocking. It's an amalgam of styrene, duck pond and dog's bed.

Hosepipes in marinas are provided on a ratio of one per half dozen berths and they are in constant demand. From portholes and forehatches, owners watch tensely, waiting to leap out and pounce the very instant a hose is free. There is always a hose-hog. He will fill his tank, every bucket, kettle and bowl, and then wash down his decks, flush out his bilges, make a paddling pool in the cockpit and, as an encore, wash two shirts, six vests and ten socks. He stops just short of colonic irrigation.

Ashore there is a drought and hosepipes are banned. At night shadowy figures top up goldfish ponds and give the beans a quick squirt while they're at it. Visiting yachtsmen, being tourists, are allowed to use water like a hydroelectric power station. Not everybody knows how to use a hosepipe. Women in general tend to converse hosepipe in hand, turning this way and that, while men leap, dodge and scream instructions. Children below the age of ten should not be allowed within 50 yards of a hosepipe. It is better to stick the nozzle down the front of your own trousers right from the start than give a child a hosepipe.

Should one be coerced into such a folly, there are rules to observe. First, lead the child to the diesel filler cap, press its nose down on it and hold it there for a count of ten while repeating distinctly the word 'NO!' Next block up every ventilator, plug the exhaust, lock both hatches, put on your boots and oilies and go ashore.

Washing up dishes is a heavy drain on water supplies. A bucket of salt water in the cockpit 'to get the worst off' is Father's favourite alternative at anchor. Marine archaeologists

21

will marvel in the future at the profusion of teaspoons to be found as a result of the cockpit wash-up. Papers will be written. Is this evidence of some sacrificial offering at the start of a voyage, a propitiation of the gods?

Just as your crofter will defend his well and the red and wriggling water supply to be found therein (which never did his granfer no 'arm, nay nor 'is fether afore 'im), so also does Old Harry defend the gruesome liquid that comes jerking up from Lord alone knows what foul depths. It would surprise nobody if fossilised Jurassic footprints were discovered in his bilges.

The kettle that chatters and bubbles dementedly and constantly on his bogey stove may well boil out the more lethal of the humours, reduce to its component parts the occasional luckless cockroach and render harmless the odd woodlouse, but it does nothing to alter its flavour.

Choose where you will, tea, coffee, cocoa all are alike. The recipient clutches his or her throat. 'GOG!' she (he) exclaims as if by way of identification. It is a touching tribute to the generosity of Old Harry that no beverage is ever served in a utensil of lesser capacity than a pint mug.

All drinks are generously sugared as standard, with the occasional exception of Bovril, and thus the consumer is left free to choose whether or not to stir it. Stirring has a similar effect to a walking stick in a garden water butt, bringing to our notice rudimentary life forms better left undisturbed.

The very fact that such creatures exist and thrive in his tank offers a fragile proof of its potability. 'You won't find none of your chemicals in there!' he affirms. Such is the turgidity of this awesome fluid, you'd be lucky to find a lost gumboot.

Well Turned Out

A good reefer jacket
Can cost you a packet
But it's under full guarantee
It can be cleaned by the draper
With blowlamp and scraper
For free.

'I take it you'll be wearing your yachting jacket' she says, any mention of trousers disturbingly omitted.

Well of course he will, what else? The yachting jacket is a maritime substitute for the lounge suit, with its faint suggestion of dilettantes lolling around on studio couches.

It is suitable wear for every social occasion from the funeral tea (ham sandwiches and 'well alright then, just another tiny drop') to howling renditions of Eskimo Nell at 1 am while draped over the club bar. In fact every occasion except yachting. Let the wearer set one foot on board and off it comes to be plastic-bagged and stuffed into the hanging locker next to her white pleats.

It must not be confused with the club blazer. Despite a nautical origin, bowls club captains in creaking surgical corsets and chest-high flannel trousers wear blazers. They have silver buttons and a pocket badge the size of a jumbo pizza. Your yachting jacket however has club buttons and it can be worn with a bewildering assortment of ties – club, regimental, school and building society.

Most wives wish their husbands would 'make more of themselves', (as if they were some sort of constructional toy having educational merit). Consequentially they retain a vested interest in a man's yachting jacket, picking lint and giving it short little tugs.

Putting anything, hands especially, in pockets is forbidden under threat of the harshest of penalties. Which means that husbands can be seen strutting around with arms extended stiffly downwards and sideways like penguins. At frequent intervals the jacket is whisked off to the dry cleaners, to be returned in a plastic sheath, stiff as a kipper and bearing a little note. *While every effort has been made to clean this garment, certain stains remain on the lapels*, it accuses, implying that the wearer has the table manners of a warthog and should stick to pelican bib, spoon and pusher.

The yachting jacket is peculiarly British. American fashion has cut off our shirt-tails and emblazoned our chests with palm trees and advertising slogans, while designer jeans grip our crotches as if about to bowl a fast spinner. But the classic lines of the great British navy-blue yachting jacket stand as a symbol of perpetual Empire and cucumber sandwiches. No other nation can copy it. American versions are in the wrong shade of navy or even (crossing ourselves) various tartans! Our Continental (apologies), our fellow-European brothers have no idea at all. You see jackets cut like a Cinzano bottle, Italians with vertical stripes and Frenchmen in shades of lime green for God's sake! The Japanese however, masters of facsimile and striving for accuracy, have produced a near-perfect version, accurate to the last gravy stain.

Cut is all-important. An unscrupulous salesman can pack you off with a décolleté neckline that leaves a lean wearer's neck looking like a turkey escaping from a basket.

'Is that comfortable round sir's hips?' queries this charlatan, flogging off a wide-skirted OS remnant. It is destined to envelop the chair back when sir sits down, thereby imparting a stiff and military bearing at table.

Our shy yachtsman may prefer to order by mail after completing a self-measurement form in the sanctity of the bathroom.

He has a diagram which shows a yachtsman, quartered like a bullock carcass and showing, unnecessarily, how to crook the elbow.

It is not always easy to complete this form with scrupulous honesty where chest measurements are concerned. Take young Percy, some people have the sea in their blood, he has cod liver oil and malt. His ribcage resembles a glockenspiel (chest measurements normal 31 in, expanded 31¾). Lacking true candour, torn between pride and precision, he ends up with a fit like a head of rhubarb under a bucket.

Once the possessor of a yachting jacket, the illusion of being smartly dressed, well-turned out, persists long after the original pristine garment has become a sagging mockery with pannier pockets and pendulous buttons. What are you going to wear, your yachting jacket? Oh, good.

Donning it lends the wearer an air of confidence. It is an instant transformation as if some stage quick-change artist, Velcro'd down the back at dizzy speed, had been propelled back on stage by an unforgiving assistant. Not even the lordly Master of Ceremonies, gingerly accepting a deckle-edged invitation card between the tips of two white-gloved fingers as if alert to the risk of anthrax or some other deadly virus, not even he can rattle the wearer of such a jacket.

Then he cops for a chair at table which is exposed to full and pitiless sunlight. His lapels are illuminated in stark detail. The encrustation of ancient nourishment would tax a forensic scientist. 'Oh look, Brown Windsor on a substrata of vindaloo...'

And there are the trousers. Beneath the sartorial splendour of the jacket the legs dwindle away to wrinkled insignificance like some genie spiralling up out of its bottle.

Being single-breasted (a designation hinting at a worrying anatomical deficiency), the yachting jacket provides little adjustment scope for the twin hazards of the best-bitter belly and bricklayer's bum. Despite skilful tailoring, it grips the buttocks (perhaps not inappropriately), like a wet towel draped over a beer barrel.

This problem is usually tackled by shifting the lower button but the time must come when, under hellish strain, it bursts free

to go winging and pinging around restaurant or salon like an angry hornet. A lady with a plunging neckline suddenly straightens up, jaws locked on chicken drumstick, eyes glazed. The time has come for a move to a *double*-breasted garment. It will have more buttons than a waiting room sofa but unlimited scope for adjustment.

A word about linings. Despite all strictures on the use of side pockets, a time of crisis must come when car key or ballpoint pierces the pocket lining. There is instant access to a wonder-world of long-lost treasures. The ticket inspector, clippers poised, waits stolidly while the scarlet-eared traveller, shoulder circling, gropes and scrabbles in the limitless depths sorting fluff, boiled sweets, small coins and other detritus amongst a mystifying tangle of sackcloth. Doubtless the reader of this utter tosh, having progressed thus far without a mention of Old Harry may feel some guarded sense of relief. It is to be short-lived.

The pride of Old Harry's wardrobe, if four nails in the back of the privy door can be dignified by this description, is undoubtedly his reefer jacket, and the cavernous wonder-world of the lining his special joy. Traditionally tailored in a fabric known as 'doeskin' (show me a navy-blue doe with brass buttons and I'm yours for life), this historic garment is of Edwardian cut and buttons up to the glottis, lending the wearer a curious resemblance to the eight of dominos. When reclining, he is eyed hopefully and hungrily by piglets and puppy dogs.

Far from being embarrassed by having easy access to the lining, he regards it as a practical asset to be exploited. This results in a wealth of objects, a cargo of useful items which combine to give him a distinctive bell-bottomed appearance. Every movement gives rise to a muffled tinkling and clunking. At social functions, crooking the elbow or reaching for some tasty canapé, produces an eerie arpeggio which sets elderly guests cursing and tapping their hearing aids.

The sheer capacity of that lining intrigues archaeologists. Resembling some newly-opened catacomb where skulls lie stacked in pyramids like some Tesco Special Offer – buy one, get one free – these scholars have to be forceably marshalled into an orderly queue.

It is also a great comfort to fellow sailors needing spares. Need a 5/16 inch shackle pin? 'Galvanised or bent and rusty?' asks a genial Old Harry. Need a dinghy bung? Here's a handful. What's this, a child in tears? No matter, here's a bullseye. The infant, instantly dry-eyed, recoils with natural wariness from this flavoursome confection. It is covered with a dense mat of fluff as if kitted out for a Russian winter.

With all the sartorial elegance of a calf in a sack, Old Harry's reefer does not escape the notice of the fashion houses of Paris and Rome, and he is always ready to offer with help and advice. He takes a firm hold on the fancy sleeves of some poor fellow who is clad in a garment of suspiciously foreign cut.

'Why, look at this!' he invites, 'single-stitched I'll be bound!' and so saying he gives a friendly albeit powerful tug.

The simple fellow is holding a Pernod in one fist and a tuna vol-au-vent in the other. They vanish as in some conjuring trick, engulfed in folds of unsatisfactory foreign fabric.

A Bit of a Drag

She says 'We're dragging!'
He shrugs off her nagging
Reassures her in accents merry
Then BLAAAAR goes a siren
The situation's a dire'n
It's the Newhaven ferry.

The hull of a yacht is like a great soundbox, responding with resonance and added volume to every whisper – a bitter truth known all too well to those with a body clock that insists on a visit to the toilet coincidental with the dishing out of cornflakes.

To the owner with a complex about dragging anchors, this phenomenon is a constant source of dread. With the company at table, trolling the jolly bowl around and exchanging humourous anecdotes, his presence whips the smiles off like Judge Jeffreys on talent night. 'QUIET!' he screams, exactly on the punch line. He had heard a little rumble. It gets so that anyone with a digestion problem (he should never have had the fried bread) reduces him to a jelly.

Anchor work takes the pea out of most whistles. Leaving an anchorage can be a dignified and unremarkable operation; a quiet slipping away to sea, unnoticed by other anchored crews and certainly inaudible. Or it can be as General Custer's Last Stand at Little Bighorn.

'I think we might do it under sail,' hazards Father, scanning the anchorage. Hearts sink. It is like Christian martyrs being told that they have just been given walk-on parts at the Coliseum. A drunk boarding a bus with a bundle of pea-sticks will cause less commotion than Father bent upon 'doing it under sail'.

To be more precise, it is a case of *almost* doing it under sail, since Father will inevitably chicken out at some stage and thump the starter button. He outlines his strategy to the stricken crew.

'We will shorten in up-and-down, weather our jib and break out on port,' he predicts rashly. The good ship *Little Hernia* bobs serenely.

Then the curtain goes up. The hands on the foredeck, flailed by a flogging jib, haul away in numb fatalism... moments later a more familiar scene is being played out. They have broken out to *starboard* and it is everybody's fault and for God's sake man 'Snub her, snub her... awwww... get out of the way. Fenders! Awwww!'

The starter button is about as much use as rubber knitting needles. 'A-wur, a-wur, a-wur,' goes the engine, on the last flicker of battery.

Lady-wife has told him fifty times, if she's told him once, that they should have had a separate battery for starting, just like everybody else. But will he listen? Oh, no! This universally acclaimed arrangement calls for a wiring diagram which is about as comprehensible to Father as cricket is to a Whirling Dervish.

'You should have got a yard man,' she's told him, implying a visit from a detective constable in shiny black boots and a belted mac. There will be a large bill for straightening out bent pulpits.

Anchoring under sail is a safer option, since Father's failing nerve during the approach results in letting go half a mile short of the anchorage. 'We're well out of all the noise and bustle here,' he states to a silent audience. Heads rise and fall to a 60 degree roll like pop-up bunnies at a fairground.

Yachting writers have valuable advice on choosing an anchorage: 'Having ascertained that anchored vessels are lying to the stream and at *full scope*, do not be afraid to place your own anchor close astern of one,' they encourage, failing to mention that such vessels may have a dinghy lying astern. There is a thump, a gurgle and a bubbling hiss. 'All gone!' proclaims Percy, giving the thumbs up.

One cannot consider the art and practice of anchoring without giving some attention to the possibility of *dragging*, the main causes of which are poor holding, inadequate scope, too small an anchor and cockpit cocktail parties.

The cheese fingers are making their fourth circuit and voices have reached a bleating crescendo, with the breaching of the second jumbo-size, Special Offer supermarket red, when a yacht is observed to be overtaking *from astern*. She has her covers on and a row of perching seagulls.

Father gives a strangled hoot and hits the starter button. The cockpit seats present a solid phalanx of legs and somewhere amongst them lies the gear lever. 'EEEEK!' trills Ms Perkins, of the rose-tinted shades and bony kneecaps, as Father's hand dives between them in search of that vital control.

The traditional dénouement with dragging anchors is an early morning confrontation of harumphing owners in their heraldic livery of Marks & Spencer pyjamas across their respective bow and stern pulpits. It smacks of garden fences and the morning after the house-warming. The owner downtide has pergola eyebrows and a moustache like a mouthful of hay. He demands that Father shall shorten his scope. If it is any shorter, the anchor will be dangling like a plumb-bob.

There is an increasing number of marina-bound owners who rate an anchor along with a fire extinguisher and fervently hope that they will never need to use either. With a full marina and condemned to 'lie outside', scope is paid out with the paucity of boarding-house jam. High tide slack and change which occurs at 0230 in a drizzle sees the predictable cabaret of bobbing torches and a bounding pyjama-clad *dramatis personae* proceeding stern-first and seaward.

From the moment he lets go, Father goes broody. His ear is cocked for every grumble and clank of chain, every creak of rope and his worried little face can be seen at any porthole like some bizarre potted savoury in a delicatessen.

In the vain hope that his anchor might be securely clamped to the sea bed, he has rigged a tripping line and buoy which will be about as handy as a cat flap in a submarine. The buoy merely acts as a sort of bait of irresistible temptation to any flophead novice who may be in search of a free visitor's buoy.

'I'll just nip up and see how she's lying,' says Father, heading deckwards for the fortieth time. His inspection reveals a yacht anchored to windward on a dubious amount of scope. Her owner's good lady is just settling down in the privacy of the cockpit, intent upon tanning her strap marks, an exercise calling for the slacking away of the various lifts and lazyjacks of female apparel. 'I don't think she's got a lot out!' notes Father critically, shading his eyes.

He will get no quarter aboard his own command. He has taken every precaution and paid out scope unstintingly. He settles into his bunk, confident of a quiet night.

'Ought you to have a last look at the anchor?' she asks. He

tries a snore. 'Oh well, if *you're* happy that it's holding, then fine!' she rasps in the darkness, thereupon falling into a deep and dreamless slumber. The doubt now planted and well watered, Father lies alert and listening. Rain drums on deck. When he gets up, he makes more row than a marching band. The ship's company lies listening, snoring theatrically.

The fouled anchor, and the attendant theatre it engenders, is an art form. 'I think I'm foul!' roars Father, uncontested.

The occasion is unmistakable. A yacht with her stern in the air and her crew in the bows staring down at nothing. The ensuing commotion invokes a sort of folklore comparable to the charming away of warts. There is reference to an absent 'tripping line' which suggests daisy chains and frilly petticoats. Father calls for a 'chain collar', hinting at some Gothic horror best not dwelt upon.

A fouled anchor may be stuck into the sea bed like a set of dentures in a church bazaar quiche. Low Water will be sometime the wrong side of midnight and it will yield suddenly, delivering on deck a black and stinking length of wire cable which pops and gibbers with obscene marine life of the lowest order.

The best that anyone can hope for is to be spared the advice, and even worse, the assistance of Old Harry – as unwelcome as the policeman's helmet to a cricket pitch streaker. An acknowledged expert in the manoeuvre of 'sailing out an anchor', it will be his first recommendation. Any owner must be counselled sternly to resist this advice.

To achieve success an anchor must be *placed* upon the sea bed with great precision, thereafter scope being fed to it promptly before it is shifted from its prescribed position. A perfect accord between helm and crew is vital. Percy is stationed on the foredeck, ready to move like a striking cobra the instant the command to let go is given. Father, drawing upon vast experience won by innumerable past cock-ups, gauges distances, speeds, tidal set and drift.

The moment has come.

'Let GO!' he cries clearly.

'Now?' enquires Percy, keen to get it right.

'Ah well, G'night all!'

'Yes, NOW!' roars Father.

The yacht drifts a couple of lengths off-site. 'I'm dropping it,' says triumphant Percy, lowering it hand-over-hand like pussy down the well. 'Say when.'

From astern come cries of wrath and an expensive scrunching noise. Percy is not to be caught out a second time. Oh-ho, no! The yacht is nearing harbour. He is already at his post in the bows. The Channel ferry is beginning to back out of her berth and Father opens the cocks up in order to get past in good time.

'What's the boy doing up there?' Mother wants to know. Father laughs indulgently. 'He's getting ready to let go, would you believe it?'

The engine is roaring.

'He's getting ready to what?' asks Mother, cocking her slightly deaf ear.

Father makes the error of a lifetime. He will wake sobbing in the night. He will develop a nervous wink which brews up still further trouble. He will for evermore roll himself up in the foetal position at the mention of anchoring.

'LET GO!' he yells fatally.

There is a rumble of chain from forward.

That Old Harry's anchor never drags comes as no surprise to those who know what he's got down there. Once he gets his best bower stuck in plus forty fathom of studlink out you're as likely to see the Arc de Triomphe going stern-first down the Seine as catch him dragging.

With that amount of iron on the sea bed he becomes a magnetic anomaly. Every magnetic compass in the locality is buzzing around like a Bendix. Passing helmsmen struggle with an eighty degree deviation and every class of vessel from a twin-berthed weekender (a double-bed with a rudder) to the Cowes ferry goes ploughing up the mud.

The wind-versus-tide phenomenon, classic excuse for dragging, gives rise to the spectacle of anchored yachts suddenly zooming to and fro at the end of their cables as if in some gigantic dance routine such as the Gay Gordons (one uses the appellation with caution having regard for the warlike qualities of that noble clan) wherein partners meet briefly and, mercifully, part before words can be exchanged.

The generosity of Old Harry's scope permits a series of great arcs and swerves to be executed. Other craft anchored nearby remain at their own risk. It is like the famed running of the bulls in Pamplona, where young men borne on pounding espadrilles hurtle by with no seats to their breeks and a ton and a half of livid bull – a forklift truck on hooves – going for gold.

To Harry it is merely an excuse for the practise of seamanlike activities such as the becket on the helm, the Worth's weight, the Prince Hammerlock moor and the deployment of kedges in every direction. The general snafu involving yachts enmeshed in the resultant web evokes no surprise. A bewildered little owner in navy knickers, having been told to dip his slack and under-run his bight, cuts himself loose and motors off thankfully.

I Heard a Little Tinkle

Tinkle, tinkle in the night
Means the stern gland isn't tight
Or that when it came to stuffin-it
You didn't put enuffin-it.

Prehistoric man, astride his log, bandy-legged and permanently soaked to the knees, was probably the last mariner not threatened by the prospect of sinking – that is until today's multi-huller – astride his inverted vessel, bandy-legged, permanently soaked to the knee and jubilantly unsinkable.

We don't give a lot of thought to the possibility of sinking, except for now and again at 0200 on a black and windy solo watch, when every wave that heaves up under the lee bow becomes a submerged container full of export garden rollers.

Today's mariners are less worried by hull leaks than their forebears, who hid their fears behind a vast and weird nomenclature. A bad leak could be *fothered* with a *thrum mat* and lesser leaks could be *maured*, a process in which a bucket of sawdust is thrust down under the leaking hull in the expectation that leaking seams would suck in beneficial quantities of the dust, which would then swell and so on. Anyone who has attempted, clandestinely, to dump gash overboard and then tried to poke it out of sight with the boathook, will appreciate the degree of skill required for this strategy.

Owners had their favourite recipes for stopping hull leaks.

35

'Have you tried porridge oats and soft soap?' enquires one, generously sharing a well-guarded secret. 'No, but I've got this nasty little dribble under my futtocks that is responding well to ground rice pudding and beeswax!' enthuses the other to a spellbound audience of fellow bus passengers.

There is also your 'hull-integrity' buff. 'I'll not have them drilling holes in *my* hull!' he trumpets, as if besieged by a squad of boatyard mateys in jungle-green boiler suits brandishing hammer-drills. With an air of defiance he proceeds to wash up the breakfast crocks in a bucket, which he then empties over the side with a tinkling of teaspoons.

Most yachts are riddled with holes like a prime Stilton, with the loo installation contributing generously to the total. The only solution is the chemical toilet – the updated 'thunderbox' dear to our ancestors. It necessitates nocturnal trips ashore to dispose of the *sealed container*.

'Excuse me, Sir!' barks HM Customs Officer, triumphantly stepping out of concealment, 'I must ask you what you have in your bag?' It is a great moment for our yachtsman.

The mechanical sea toilet is the bane and dread of the tyro, living afloat for the first time. It seems that one cannot have an ordinary, simple bowel movement without manipulating all manner of levers, cocks, pumps and gate valves. It is like starting up a fairground steam organ. All it lacks is the smirking plaster shepherdess banging cymbals.

'Shhh, I thought I heard a little tinkle!' says Blanche, raising a cautionary finger.

Father is on to it like a hound from the slips. He wrenches open the loo door. His bowl it doth run over. He proceeds to give the most moving performance of his thespian career afloat. With his features wrenched into a mask of intolerable suffering, he calls upon his Maker to bear witness. 'Why?' he flutes. 'We could all have been drowned as we slept!' The unlikely event of people sleeping blissfully while being immersed slowly in a freezing English Channel escapes him. The guilty party will bear the mark of Cain for life, pointed out in the street in whispers, as might a reprieved mass-murderer.

When it comes to sinking, boats need no help from us. They can manage very nicely unaided. Just as the humble bank vole, toiling away underground at the plastic liner to an ornamental garden pool, can turn that charming feature into a puddle of stinking mud and dead goldfish, so too can the yacht left on moorings provide a rude surprise for her owners returning at the weekend.

Father gets out of the car and shades his eyes. 'Oh, deary me!' he chuckles with good-natured tolerance for the ineptitudes of fellow mariners. 'Some poor swine is in for a nasty shock, eh?' He surveys the distant mast, 6ft of which is protruding from the water. His smile slowly stiffens as though it had been varnished on. His Adam's apple rises and falls once... 'Did we leave the burgee up?' he asks generally, in stricken tones.

There are such time-honoured sources of leak as the stern gland. Like some holy well deep in its grotto, haunt of naiad and shy kingfisher, it never runs dry and is seldom visited. The ritual of 'hardening it down' is one bitterly familiar to many a sailing wife, whose job it will be to hand tools to her spouse and suffer his clicks and sighs at being handed the wrong one.

The disembodied knees, shins and toe-blasted deck shoes, visible in the deep and shadowy recesses of the quarter berth, are not the grisly evidence that some maniacal meat-saw killer has been at work, but Father attending to the stern gland.

The time will come when merely screwing down the greaser and causing more worms of grease to writhe into the bilge is not enough; it will have to be repacked. The shaft has been rattling around like a walking stick down a gutter. Torch in mouth and one-handed, ring spanner to full stretch of finger tips, Father howls for yet another as it joins the rest in the deep vee of the sterntuck. Short of training his five-year-old on a Lego mock-up in the cupboard under the kitchen sink, he will have to 'Get the yard in!' which, for your budget owner, is near to blasphemy.

The boatyard, forbidden by the Factories Act to stuff apprentices down black holes as if rabbiting with a ferret, solves the problem by lifting out the engine – a process which will cost about the same as a gas chairman's salary.

Another ritual of modern yachting relates to the 'log impeller skin fitting', a term smacking of cosmetic surgery and a bit of slack around your wattles. At the end of a cruise, and prior to leaving the boat, it has to be *unshipped*, an exercise akin to applying a thumb over one of the mighty fountains of Versailles.

It's a chore traditionally reserved for Father, who privately dreads it. The job involves unscrewing and withdrawing the impeller and replacing it with a screwcap. With the cabin sole up, Father, sleeves rolled, kneels by the hole as if in deep mourning at a graveside. Blanche stands by with basin, swabs and a towel. He has thought out a new system. This time he will hold the cap in his right hand while unscrewing the impeller with his left. He slackens off a few turns, grits his teeth and the old familiar spluttering howl of dismay rises from the forehatch as he lifts his ravaged and dripping features to the light.

The throbbing heart of a boat used to be the bilge pump. In days when deckheads dripped like Mother Shipton's Grotto, and hull seams munched their oakum as if it were some new health breakfast cereal, you relied on your bilge pump.

Typical might be Old Harry's converted winkle walloper, a vessel with the windward qualities of a nun's bonnet. Although never a class of craft to quicken the pulse and bring a lump to the throat (apart from the occasion when he boiled the sink plug with the potatoes), she had a pump barrel that could woo a potholer and a pump well with an echo. You had to lower a canary in a cage prior to groping for the lost starting handle; if you had fallen down, you would have needed a decompression stop on the way up.

The pump handle, shipped in a deck socket next to the black maw of the open barrel, looks like an iron heron peering down in expectation of being richly rewarded. It has never disappointed. Slurp-clunk, slurp-clunk went the pump and at each stroke a reeking black scum burped up over the sidedeck. It was peppered with dead beetles, lentils, dog-ends, blanket fluff and unidentifiable gobbets of corruption.

Not so your light displacement go-go boat of today, in which a pint of water goes everywhere, like a puddle next to a bus stop. None of your cast-iron artifacts here. Oh no. In a pump well the size of dolly's bath there is an electronic sensor. Like some electronic big toe, recoiling from contact with rising water, it motivates a softly humming pump which quickly copes with the emergency. Excepting just that once...

The sleeper, alerted by the chilliness on his buttocks, awakens and raises himself upon one elbow. As though taking a salute at some naval review, he watches his shoes go floating past.

A Touch Astern

Charge into the berth
For all you're worth
With a bit of panache
The trick is to learn
When to bang her astern.
CRASH!

The prospect of manoeuvring under engine within the narrow confines of harbour or marina is one which keeps many a novice owner uneasy in his bed. 'You should never have had the rissoles,' his wife accuses, bouncing steadily on her side of the mattress as he revolves unendingly on his. 'Should I put the helm hard over and open the throttle wide, or should I go ahead-and-astern?' he agonises. Either option promises to be richly rewarding for onlookers. The hand hovers above the gear lever as if about to detonate a factory chimney.

We yachting writers expound copiously on the subject. 'Do you know your turning circle?' we sneer, drawing one in dotted lines, in case somebody doesn't know what a circle looks like. 'Once you know your turning circle you can proceed with confidence. Having started your turn *do not waver,*' we encourage. In other words, if you are going to hit the refuelling barge, hit it head on and hit it *hard*.

The fact that turning circles are usually banana-shaped, and alter in size according to wind, current and the apoplectic screams of the Harbourmaster, tends to escape the notice of the writer at the helm of a word processor. We have not, as yet, even considered the effects of the dreaded astern gear.

Father commences his turn, relaxed and smiling. He has visited this marina before and his manoeuvre on that occasion was a little gem, subject to admiring congratulations from all sides. His hand rests lightly upon the helm. Then at some point while approaching the apogee of his (elliptical) circle, his knuckles whiten, eyeballs begin to protrude like church mission coat-pegs and his smile becomes the mirthless rictus of a rocking horse. His pipe stem snaps like a dry twig. He chickens out and bangs the gear lever from full ahead to hard astern. 'Wheee!' howls the gearbox. 'Ooooo!' exclaim onlookers in excited anticipation.

Father's modest intention had been to berth his boat smoothly and efficiently with minimum fuss, quiet and unhurried, *professionally*. Had he entered harbour dressed as a hobbyhorse and blowing a cardboard trumpet, he could hardly have attracted more unwanted attention. From the Harbour Office, a loud-hailer crackles into life. 'Harrump, gag, dronkit gondrome!' it roars commandingly. Our mariner at this point has his vessel wind-up-tail and in the narrow bit.

She is revolving prior to going into the dreaded zigzags. Mother, knowing the signs, has gone below to put on the Brussels sprouts.

It is always unnerving, while carrying out a manoeuvre, to note what people ashore are doing. If it is going well, then probably nobody will notice the fact. When pedestrians suddenly stop and shade their eyes, when shopkeepers come to stand in their doorways, and when the cockpits of moored yachts suddenly fill with spectators, it is high time to do something drastic, like clutching the throat and falling to the deck with rolling eyeballs, or handing over the con to Percy.

'I mustn't hog the helm. Here lad, try your hand at a simple manoeuvre.'

Engine manufacturers seem bent upon unsettling the mariner's already shaky confidence. 'When did you last dip your sump/renew your impeller/replace your filters, eh, EH? Tell me that! And how about your alternator belt?' they sneer.

Perhaps the keenest test of equanimity is the auxiliary engine, which has to be stopped and then started again to achieve reverse gear. It is like asking a tightrope walker to produce his bus pass when halfway across Niagara Falls. He stops, lays down his balancing pole, begins patting pockets. 'I have it here... somewheeeeeeahhh!'

Over-confidence wreaks its own dire punishment and the gear lever imposes it. A stately procession of cardinals, under full sail and approaching a rag rug on a polished parquet floor, promises a spectacle of equal interest to Father, *who likes to brief his crew in advance* of a manoeuvre.

'I shall circle once to assess the situation and then lay my port side to,' he explains, implying that he will do so personally and alone, levitating, perhaps, or maybe skimming round in a yogic flight knees akimbo. He then proceeds to do something entirely different. It is a situation akin to an ant's nest disturbed by the gardener's fork. Tiny creatures clutching eggs hurry hither and yon in fear. Crew, clutching fenders, scuttle to and fro across the coachroof with comparable urgency.

The ultimate test of nerve and skill is to lie alongside the fuelling berth just after the lock gates have opened. For the tyro it is a folly as rich in potential disaster as attempting an after-dinner speech, owlish on club claret and containing the words 'auspicious occasion'.

The aim is to hover, ready to make a dive for the berth as soon as the present incumbent quits it. Half a dozen yachts circle very slowly while half a dozen wives hiss instructions from as many companionways. 'NOW, Gerald!' rasps a voice. Then the boat owner in the berth decides to take on water as well, and too late, *too late*, Gerald (who has gunned his engine) hits the astern gear. Saint Peter, patron saint of boatmen, places hand over eyes and shudders.

Dead astern, a vast powerboat bubbles and burbles like simmering porridge. High on her flying bridge stands her owner wearing a paisley cravat of pneumatic perfection. Father, looking up his nostrils with distaste, also wears a cravat. His looks like a surgical dressing.

The tremendous thirst of the powerboat's twin what-ever-they-ares will mean a tip of commensurate size for the fuel attendant. Father will want a five-gallon top-up dribbled in as though administering eardrops. He gets the blind eye treatment. He won't be treated like that! By God, no! He'll go somewhere else, won't he? Like rowing ashore with a jerry can when the tank ran dry. Two miles through drizzle, then bleed the engine when he gets back. THAT showed 'em.

A series of shattering bangs and barking mechanical eructations herald the arrival under power of Old Harry in his converted whelk pilliker. Somewhere ashore a retired SAS man kicks in a door and shields are issued to riot police. Lacking the refinement of a gearbox, Old Harry relies upon his own unique sense of judgement when approaching a berth, stopping his thumping monolith with a screwdriver across plug and block and carrying his considerable way thereafter in total silence.

In World War Two, the arrival of the dreaded 'buzz-bomb' was typified by the cut-out of its throaty growl – silence – and then a mighty explosion. This eerie silence followed by detonation also typifies Old Harry's arrival in the berth of his choice.

Like rabbits mesmerised by a stoat, yacht crews destined to receive this horrific visitor watch saucer-eyed. A pitch pine bowsprit, like some witch doctor's accusing finger, points unerringly. 'It could be YOU!' it seems to proclaim. Then comes frantic activity as a wealth of fenders are produced.

Old Harry's rope-clad motor tyres promise little comfort. Chins are squared. Men stand ready with little tubular boathooks and one crew jumps ship *en bloc*, led by a Junoesque lady who looks like a Samurai warrior in her foundation garments.

The Harbourmaster, who had rashly declared that Old Harry would enter the marina under sail 'Over my dead body', was later coaxed out from under his desk with a chocolate bourbon. He was sparing in his comments. 'Mummy, mummy!' he lisped, crawling back again.

Around the Ragged Rock

Having rounded the Fastnit
You'll forget that you're past-it
You'll forget the hiding you've taken
But recall with dread
That bit of fried bread
And fatty bac'n.

There are still yachtsmen to be found who think that Fastnet Rock is lettered all the way through and thereby provides a low-budget gift to take home to mother for looking after the cat.

These are the poor swine who have never propped their stubbled chins on the lee dodger while their little vessel plunges around it in a streaky dawn and a wet Force 6. There will be the sort of sea running beloved of 18th-century Dutch marine artists.

Once round that Rock and they are changed men. 'Fastnet!' they grit, with a harsh laugh and a bitter quirk. 'Well nothing... really.' They don't like to talk about it. When pressed, 'By heaven it was *hell* out there!' They grunt, struggling to control a nervous tic. The application of a lighted cigarette end is the best way to control tics.

But your Fastnet veteran never admits to winds that reach gale status. They may have been reefed down to headboard and clew cringle, he may get home with a bit of seaweed over his port earhole as a result of rounding the Scillies a bit tight, but as for wind, 'Oh it freshened a bit during the night', he demurs modestly.

Not so your first-timers. 'Is it a gale, is it a gale?' they tweet, seeking credibility for the monstrous and howling lies they will tell when they get home.

'Well there we were...' they begin. The room clears as if you'd lit a sulphur candle.

It starts, reasonably enough, with the start. Quite a normal start. There is the owner on the helm (to the unspoken disapproval of his entire crew) white of face, dewlaps a'tremble, staring around him in deep apprehension like Alice in Wonderland confronted by the homicidal Duchess.

'Where's the line, where's the line?' he whinnies to the deaf crew. They pack the cockpit stiff, all waving winch handles to justify their presence on deck at this critical time.

A gigantic Admiral's Cupper comes slicing up. Her helmsman has the square-jawed and forbidding mien of Metal Micky; she is crewed by neckless titans with vast buttocks who are all winding things, apparently with concentrated hate.

'How long have I got, how long have I got?' whimpers our owner.

Just about long enough to commend your soul to your Creator mate if that lot clouts them... which sounds like some sort of buy-one-get-one-free Special Offer.

They make a start like Moses leading the faithful into the wilderness. The owner's clever manoeuvre (he read an article), sets them back like all snakes and no ladders. There is a long and uneasy period of silence. The owner clears his throat.

'Well we've got our wind clear anyway!' he bleats in defiance. So did Moses, plus endless empty miles of goddam sand.

Watches having been drawn, the small vessel settles down into her racing mode. Crew members are either prone and groaning resonantly into buckets or steering with haggard concentration. It will be alright once they get their sea legs, they comfort each other, implying some sort of optional extra to be delivered by Parcel Force.

With Class I long since hull-down on the horizon ahead, the remainder settle to battling it out with a personal rival of comparable ineptitude – either a contender for line honours in some local club where the Points Aggregate Teaspoon is at stake or another owner who still has his own hair, still charms the ladies and drives a bigger 4x4.

The race follows the usual pattern. They vomit their way from The Needles to Start Point with pockets full of water and Cream Cracker mush, then the wind goes flat calm simultaneously with the tide going foul. They all kedge. A dead crab nods by followed by something long, plastic and highly suspect. Hours later, with the speedo needle struggling to get off the stop mark, the race is on again. With the better part of four hundred miles to go it will be free bus passes and Zimmer frames all round by the time they cross the line. Typically by 3 am there will be coachroof and foredeck heroics to reduce sail. The owner, alone in the cockpit, howls orders to himself and Percy staggers in circles with his cap hammered down over his jug ears. Every inch of space below is suddenly packed with sodden sailcloth.

Then off they roar Rockwards. The owner goes below 'to look at the chart', as if it had some sudden and special significance. (It has. It is the only dry thing in the ship). He lies down to consider race strategy and falls into a healthy nightmare; they are sailing over a raging sea of torn-up fivers.

There was a bad moment off the Longships when they found three metres on a dodgy echo sounder and hove-to in order to take a sounding with a ring spanner on a string (which they lost) and there was the run back from the Rock.

In a driving murk, the visibility of a transport caff and Force 8 up the chuff there are some tense moments as they approach the Bishop. With more crosses on the chart than a garden trellis the owner takes to his RDF to confirm position.

'Let's see if we can pick it up,' he muses, twiddling. He staggers to his feet tearing off his headphones as if they were red hot. 'Gybe, gybe, gybe her!' he howls, his little boots scrabbling on the companionway steps. Then comes the traditional run back from the Bishop with the lee-berth jockeys now risen from the dead and keen to battle it out with rivals coming up fast from astern.

The owner trains his binos. 'Ho-ho so they want to play huh!' he chuckles dangerously. There is a mounting Force 7.

Flying Mallard is roaring up still under her spinnaker, which is jammed aloft and won't come down. Her owner is down below, jibbering in stark terror and with a pillow on his head.

Our owner, never the man to resist a challenge, orders his own spinny to be set. It is like hitching a tow from the Tokyo Bullet train. Both yachts go tearing up-Channel, totally out of control, straight past Plymouth, the Prizegiving Dinner fill-'em-up, fill-'em-up and on. Eventually they become dismasted hulks astern of the Newhaven Lifeboat.

No Fastnet Race is complete without the comforting presence of Old Harry in his converted Cleethorpes Whitebait Shoveller, ready with advice and hints for all – received by competitors with the guarded enthusiasm they might show for a Caesar Borgia cookbook.

While not actually in the race (his TCF would net him a start a fortnight ahead of everybody else), his presence at the start and at intervals along the route is the signal for competitors to give him the sort of wide berth granted to flag-sellers outside supermarkets.

The ten-minute gun triggers off a harrowing period for race officers. His appearance on the line being akin to the arrival of a chippy van on the lawn at Glyndebourne (salt 'n vinegar guv?) and a double wrapping of the *Sun*. The race officer, blinking rapidly in disbelief, rubs the object lens of his binos hoping thereby to dislodge the monstrous foreign body apparently blocking his view.

Thereafter, Old Harry is to be seen barrelling up and down the line howling comment and advice to those lucky enough to win his attention, while his bowsprit twangs fore and backstays like some gigantic lady harpist, all bun, bum and black satin.

There was one historic occasion when he actually held down a crewing job for the duration of a race – a feat smacking of half-nelsons and Cornish wrestlers in leather jockstraps. It was a pierhead jump with all the potential of a high dive and a low tide. There was this nervous little owner at the bottom of Class Everything who had been lucky enough to buy this second-hand racer, an amazing offer never-to-be-repeated on threat of imprisonment.

Old Harry, waving a CV that would have made Joshua Slocum blush, came aboard to fill a gap in the crew list. A sheet of corrugated iron would have been better and handier in the cockpit. What with his ankle length, storm-fronted oily coat well larded with Cape Horn dressing, his hurricane trousers, cork preserver and a sou'wester like a chicken coop, he made a stirring sight. He was a monument to cork and callosity and carrying a sea bag like a dead tup. A wardrobe on a wheelbarrow would have been more useful on deck. Accustomed to roomier vessels he blocked both companion and forehatch, thus rendering any sail change a distressing and distasteful experience for those stationed below and therefore compelled to dismantle his ensemble from the bottom upwards.

So he was nominated cook. Crew gazed in numb fascination at the greasy bonanza that lay shuddering on their plates. 'That'll stand by yer,' he promised. 'That'll lie a'nourishin'yer all night long!'

So he was nominated navigator. They hit the Fastnet Rock bang on. It was lucky he just happened to have this double-thrummed collision mat in his sea bag.

A Hard Line to Take

If you don't insist
On a monkey's fist
Your line won't go very far
But make sure that it
Is covered with grit
Sump oil, red lead and tar.

Apart from those laconic professional deckies and dockies who still hurl ropes at one another, the Proper Yachtsman's Heaving Line went out with wing collars and the broderie anglaise modesty front. Beer was tuppence a pint and paid hands stunned one another to rocking stupefaction by hurling these hempen missiles at point-blank range.

Heaving and receiving was an art learned painfully but it sharpened up the footwork a treat. No myopic explorer hanging his solar topee on the horn of the glowering rhinoceros ever moved so fast.

We need look no further than Old Harry for examples of prime heaving lines. They vary from clock-spring sisal and dripping coir, with its vile marine population of hopping, wriggling life forms, to a rank and reeking coil which has been dressed with fish oil to render it as limp as a literary luncheon handshake. Each will terminate in a sort of woven cannonball, the so-called monkey's fist. Show me the monkey with fists of that calibre and it is welcome to pick the cherry off my cake any day of the week mate.

With the solidity of a frozen cricket ball, it is like a monstrous fruit from some steaming and fever-ridden jungle, concealing a 'pip' consisting of a rusty 1¼ inch whitworth nut. The sagging jibs of dockside cranes bear vivid witness to his source of supply. The addition of an annual coat of white enamel builds up an impregnable and armour-piercing carapace.

Old Harry's heaving lines are regarded as offensive weapons by the police. There should be a national amnesty so that they could be handed in. They could be photographed by the press, held up for inspection by a copper of high rank.

'We are determined to outlaw this menace from the terraces!' he might thunder. He drops it with a dull and sickening thump on his toe and exits howling in a series of spectacular bounds.

It was not until the first synthetic warp came bubbling out of its test tube that the fate of the old-time heaving line was finally sealed and we began hurling the new lightweight, high-thingummy, low whatnot synthetic warps at each other. We miss at our peril and at the cost of ten feet of toe rail.

Distinction must be made between the throwing line, which has a hard rubber quoit on the end and a compassionate function – it can be hurled great distances in the wrong direction or in expert hands score a ringing welt around the earhole of the casualty – and the heaving line per se.

A heaving line cannot be bought Vac-U-Packed with instructions in Arabic and Japanese and sanitised for your protection. It must be *made up*. Nowadays a few home-made, featherweight heaving lines may survive here and there, although heaving *bundle* might be a fairer description and delivery by sugar tongs a safer means of propulsion.

Such 'heaving lines' serve a number of functions. Miriam wants to 'rinse out a few things' (a carefully low-key description of the clandestine rape of the water tank). Danger raises its grisly head when Percy falls overboard. Father brooks no delay.

'Keep cool, keep cool, heaving line, heaving line!' he squeals, implying that carbon copies are required. His eye remains fixed upon the threshing Percy in accordance with The Book.

His outstretched hand behind him gropes for the vital line.

Percy takes delivery of a colourful assortment of knickers, bras, string vests and tea towels with more astonishment than gratitude.

The throwing of ropes is fundamental. The departing ocean liner linked to the land by gay paper streamers symbolises the deeply emotional nature of departure. Loved ones watch misty-eyed. Features work convulsively, upper lips stiffen and choking sobs are heard.

The arrival of a yacht with her broadside of ropes evokes similar reactions. On the quay, lips move in silent prayer. Choking grunts signify emotions of heartfelt gratitude for her safe return. Let us consider a typical case.

The novice on the foredeck, bouncing on the balls of the feet in the Wimbledon shuffle, making small, threatening swings with his coil. On the quay the recipient dodging and feinting like a goalie. Unlike this maligned player however, who, having let one through, glares around in hauteur and dignified indignation, our lad will take full responsibility for having missed. 'Oh, God. Sorry!' he cries, a sinner seeking absolution.

WHAM! The second attempt brings penance and absolution in one handy bite-size package.

A word on the art of receiving a line. It can be like being the patsy in a knife-throwing act minus the mirthless smile and fishnet stockings. There are times when the only assistance ashore may be the brightly attired holidaymaker, hung about with little plastic pouches containing photographic trivia and watching the advancing yacht expectantly as if about to witness a total eclipse. He should be viewing the proceedings through smoked glass.

The gap between ship-and-shore vanishes like trying to save a place in a bus queue.

'I say. Will you take my line please?' quavers our tyro.

The first shot, yo-yo-like, falls at his feet, the next brings up 0.0006 mm from the muffin's clutching fingers and the third hits the pontoon and slithers back into the water. He dives for it

with the speed of a striking hawk, crushing his accoutrements and grabbing the rope-end whipping between finger and thumb.

'Make it FAST!' screams our lad. He can't go no faster, squire.

The classic problem though is this: who makes what fast? A knowledgeable yachtsman on the jetty or quay with a cap badge and tufts of hair in his ears like a squirrel may wish to take charge. Or both make fast their ends. Or both let their ends go. It is like watching a failed conjurer eyeing the premature release of disgruntled doves.

With engine screaming full astern the yacht grinds shuddering and screeching up the transom of the boat in front as in some gargantuan mating ritual.

Up Aloft with Old Harry

Old Harry's arrivals are dreaded by harbourmasters the length of the coast, who would as soon face a howling mob of fuzzy-wuzzies. On his approach, they at once appoint a deputy in the person of The Lad, a pink-cheeked and downy-chinned adolescent, innocent as Miss Muffit, who is still not above a secret romp with his Action Men.

Beaming with pride at this sudden and dizzy promotion, the lad spits on his palms and adopts a wicketkeeper's crouch.

'Righty-ho, Sir' he trebles, fatally. 'LET ME HAVE IT!'

A Well-oiled Clack

In the fitting out season
The weather is freezin'
You munch your lunch in the lee
With frozen toes
And a dripping nose
Going plinkity plonk in your tea.

'You haven't forgotten my coffee morning have you?' she says.

Why of course he hasn't! Why else would he have the stepladders on the roof rack and his folding workbench in the boot, and why would he be wearing the jeans with more paint on them than the ceiling of the Sistine Chapel? It is the first dry Saturday in two months and don't blame him if they have to pay the yard to antifoul her that's all!

He will find that he is in charge of Guessing the Number of Seeds in the Seedcake stall. Several of the ladies remark that he is looking a bit peaky. Eric Bloodaxe probably looked a bit peaky when he was sacking Scarborough.

The husband who neglects his home jobs in favour of the boat is treading a wobbly tightrope. He repairs the garden gate hinge with string.

'That'll hold it for the time being' he affirms.

Your forest traveller holding shut the muzzle of a furious wolf shares a similarly short stay of wellbeing.

Ideally, fitting out should be an activity for all the family and, as the old saying goes, 'the family that fits out together ends up being investigated by Social Services'.

A family working party ('Don't argue with me boy you're coming!') radiates fun like a solemn convocation of Cardinals. Sandra pines for her stable-dung shovel and The Boy slumps as if he'd been filleted. Mother tackles the galley and toilet, sorrowing over that stain, while on deck the kids squawk away at rock-hard varnish with blunt scrapers in a withering nor'-easter. Father does something highly technical and out of the wind.

There is this strongly defended belief, held by men, that they are born with a God-given mechanical aptitude, a blessed gift giving them the ability to drive nails in straight and prise lids off tins. Women, in their opinion, are 'good at cakes'. Accordingly, while women scrape, scrub and rub, men attend to such hi tech tasks as applying masking tape and making brown-paper gaskets.

They use technical terms to heighten the mystery. Father completes his diagnosis of the bilge pump. A pierced diaphragm would have been bad enough but... 'I've got a sticky clack, Muriel!' he mourns.

'Oh you poor darling. Sit down!' she murmurs.

Loading up the car for the long drive to the boat calls for deep concentration. There must be no interruption while he checks his list.

'Rat-tail file, 2ba box spanner, eight inch brass roundheads..' he intones.

'Egg-and-tomato alright dear?' Muriel prompts.

'Stilson wrench, emery paper, wire to poke down loo..'

'... Because last time you said the skins got under your top set..'

'Antifouling and brush, thinners, masking tape..'

'...Or maybe you'd rather have egg-and-cucumber?'

The car ends up trimmed by the stern and loaded like a Bedouin camel.

'Everybody aboard!' cries father merrily. 'New loo seat, Araldite, graphite, Loc-tite and hold tight all!' He engages first gear.

'Everything except the kitchen sink, eh!', he comments humourously. He should have added 'and the boat keys'.

The amount of work you can do in a short winter's day is modest and getting started is the first obstacle. It may be a day of sparkling sunshine but down below there is a permafrost lacking only a frozen mammoth. A newly opened tomb is cosier. One expects a row of grinning skulls like Toby jugs. Coffee would be nice. The gas bottle is frozen and the instant coffee jar contains a shrunken nub like a fossil.

Or maybe it is raining, and the first couple of hours are spent in the steamy frowst of a transport caff. The sky clears. Back at the boat Father climbs aboard. 'I think we did the right thing by staying dry!' he opines, flinging back the winter cover. A Niagara descends upon the upturned faces below.

Quantity boatbuilding production methods call for the engine and the loo to be fitted before the deck is added, which is like hanging the pictures before the roof goes on. It spells aggro for the amateur artisan.

The weepy stern gland (an ailment suggesting social embarrassment) can only be got at by a pixie in a little red hat. Mother, knowing full well the cursing, sighing and bellowing which will go on if Father tries it, forestalls this.

'You'd better get the yard to look at it', she says flatly. One imagines the entire staff from MD to canteen cat lining up for a peep.

Equally difficult is the job that needs to be done in the confines of the loo or the aptly named 'hanging locker', where the worker can insert an arm and a shoulder, one buttock or a head but never all at once. While hands grope unseen the face wears an expression of remote vacuity, like a French accordionist or a RADA student doing homework.

Work below decks calls for forethought, and lacking it Father moves from job to job in mounting frustration. Where are his spare clacks and his circlip pliers? He looks around for a scapegoat. Mother busies herself sorting lockers. 'Psaaaw!' she says carrying something on deck between finger and thumb. She begins collecting last season's emergency stores.

These have been rattling around all summer and the tins look like something from the Gokstadt Ship Fund. 'Best before July 10th' state the labels guardedly. This is a manufacturer's way of saying get it down you before August because it will be luminous and ticking by September. Father hasn't seen the last of them.

Emergency stores will greet him daily on his return from the office. Tinned pilchards (leviathans in tomato sauce) will appear and reappear again and again in a variety of forms like some private dick in a series of baffling disguises. There is the Uncle Ben's Rice, Wunda cake mix and packets of Muggasoup all in suspiciously rotund packets.

Work on the topsides, once calling for the holy zeal and dedication of Church Guild ladies embroidering hassocks and cassocks, is now a mere matter of applying some gloop with a moist cloth and small circular strokes. Removes obstinate stains the tin lies shamelessly. The marvel is that yachtsmen have yet to attract the TV admen.

'Game for the Topsides Challenge?' taunts the presenter, waving his pack of Toppo. He raps on the hull and the owner pops up as though propelled by a charge of guncotton. Then there's 'brightwork', nowadays we are down to 'teak trim', crafted in genuine wood. You can either go for a bare teak effect by scrubbing it (once, when you've just bought the boat), oiling it, which means a sprinkling over the entire deck and coachroof as though bestowing a blessing, or varnishing.

When the final gloss coat has been applied by Father (and who else?), he stands back to admire his work, a man fulfilled. This is the signal for every power-sander, scratching dog, swarm of flies and moulting sparrow over a five mile radius to converge on the boat.

A worse menace is the Sunday Drinks. It will be a perfect varnishing day. At breakfast there is a silence you could cut up into small chunks. 'I'm warning you', she says, 'Just don't start, that's all!' When did they last go out together, eh? Tell her that!

Sunday Drinks parties occupy the time slot between the

morning dew drying off and the afternoon dew beginning to fall. They are a sort of social watering hole where lion and gazelle sip guardedly, alert for turkey-necked old crocodiles in unsuitably brief black frocks.

With Old Harry's vessels always being in a state of permanent disintegration, his fitting out season is ongoing. 'There's always some little finishin' touch needing to be looked at,' he laughs wryly, nipping aside as some massive item of rigging crashes on deck. He looks at it.

Flying a Kite

Some people are finniky
About setting the spinniky
This is a common failing
And when they gybe-them
One can only describe them
As gift-wrapped and
Ready for mailing.

Father eyes a passing Admiral's Cupper with sour envy. To a man, her crew wear sweatbands, and their minuscule shorts bulge with muscle; they glare around through narrowed eyes. He steals an uncharitable glance at his own foredeck powerhouse.

There is brother-in-law Norman, whose knobbly little knees give him the appearance of cane furniture – or, notes Father, warming to his theme, perhaps in those bell-bottomed shorts, more like the bamboo and inverted flowerpot arrangement of an earwig trap. There is also Nance's Boy, with the jug ears and xylophone ribcage, who is outgrowing his strength.

Setting a spinnaker with a crew of that calibre is not the sort of thing to be undertaken lightly. Yet some go for it in the same twice-a-summer spirit of devilry that prompts a garden barbecue. It takes place the day after a three-week heatwave, and is enlivened by a thunderstorm, a doused grill and a power cut.

This does not prevent him from prowling the boatyard at fitting out time offering advice and assistance to those less fortunate than himself. His appearance is like watching swimmers quit the water upon the approach of the telltale triangular fin. Within seconds they have scuttled into their loos and banged and bolted their doors.

Old Harry, listening at a skin fitting, raps on the hull. He clears his throat and addresses the soil-pipe outlet in the lofty and strangulated tones usually associated with answerphone messages.

'Did you know you have gribble up your tuck?' he enquires alarmingly. To the cowering owner of a GRP hull he reveals the true versatility of his knowledge. Was the owner aware, he wants to know, that he had a nasty patch o' Hoss Moses up his trunk? No problem, just leave it to him...

'No no. Go away!' sobs the owner in vain.

Too late. Old Harry is already hefting his bent file scraper and pumping up a huge and lethal petrol blowlamp... He strikes a match.

But let's face it – as the big game hunter said when the rogue elephant placed a foot on the tail of his solar topee – good maintenance is what really matters, stripping things down, lightly oiling and then reassembling them back-to-front.

'My galley pump has never been the same since you made it work!' accuses Muriel, lifting vengeful and dripping features.

> *All for the lack of a well-oiled clack*
> *Many a ship has sunk*
> *Instead of a gush there's a horrible hush*
> *Then the pump gives a horrible CLUNK.*

A Session with the Bottles

They cost two hundred quid
These binoculars did
They're designed to float-look
GULP! Quick, get the boathook.

'*Somebody* must try to win this race!' grizzles the owner, waving aside food and drink. The implication is that anybody else taking nourishment is in some way squandering their chances, indulging in bacchanalian delights denied the serious racing man. Jaws in mid-chomp freeze on cold chicken drumstick – Neanderthal Man preserved for all time in glacial ice. He thrusts his unshaven muzzle up into the cockpit where he notes that the wind is now right aft and the genoa is still strapped in like a straightjacket. He puts on his special and infuriating Little Lord Fauntleroy voice.

'Oh please don't anybody move... carry on eating... I'm sure I can set the spinny singlehanded, stow the genny and bag it.'

For the past couple of hours, while the owner snored resonantly below, the crew have been grunting and straining through a succession of headsail changes and as many wind shifts. There is a furious rattle of expectorated drumsticks. They begin crashing around in a savage burlesque of efficiency. There is an atmosphere like somebody just boiled the milk over.

This is the moment chosen by Percy, on his first race, to make his appearance on deck. Our hitherto horizontal young hero has timed his return to the land of the living with a degree of ineptitude comparable to attending a funeral wearing a joke bow tie.

'I think I might just manage a Cream Cracker now.' He tells the owner.

He has just booked himself a spell with the bottles.

In any offshore racing fleet, as sleek ocean greyhounds 'o the deep plunge headlong into the roaring billows and plastic detritus, a keen observer might notice that some carry a prone figure right up in the bows, hooded and cursing, with binoculars clamped to streaming features. He is 'having a spell with the bottles', keeping a lookout for sail numbers and keeping the hell out of it where he can do the least harm and might even be of some minuscule bit of use for God's sake. 'K one-eight-six' he wails, spitting salt and to the birds.

He is a tyro, a bumble-bum newcomer to the racing scene, the boss's son, the wife's brother from Canada or the brother's wife from who-the-hell-cares anyway. Tyros foul up short-tacking like barbed wire in a bag of knitting. They steer as if the wheel was a test-your-grip machine and what they can do to a spinnaker gybe has reduced bucko mates to a state of thumb-sucking shock beneath the chart table.

Percy, having excelled in all these instances *and* taken to the lee settee berth while hard on the wind instead of lying clamped to the weather berth like a house martin under the eaves in a proper seamanlike manner, regards his dispatch to the foredeck as some gratifying form of promotion.

He has a mooring cleat in his navel and his elbows lodged in a couple of fairleads. It is a posture that leaves his oily sleeves open to the heavens and an unbroken deluge of salt water. It exits via his trouser zip like a lawn sprinkler. Through his 12 x 50s he observes a dizzy and hazy world wherein huge objects swoop and zoom to and fro like staff nurses ejecting visitors. 'Two-three-five-PSAAW!' he howls desolately.

There comes a long spell without sightings and, due to the owner's inspired hunch that there is to be a wind shift, they put in a five-mile hike out to sea. 'Well it won't catch us out lads!'

he opines, tapping his nose. Six hours later, in a steady wind, they begin catching up the Class Three walking wounded.

'I've got one, I've got one!' rejoices Percy.

'Shut that fool up!' snarls the owner.

Not every owner will lend his bottles so freely, of course. Most cherish them with the jealous anxiety of a collector of fine art having his Rubens dusted. When a visitor's child hangs them around his tiny bull neck and blunders around swinging them like Magog laying waste with his club, his pitiful falsetto cries would bring a tear to the sternest eye.

In years gone by The Owner's Binocular was usually gigantic, ensuring a rapid descent to the sea bed for any wearer misguided enough to fall overboard. Such an instrument, ex-WW2, had usually seen service in the Tank Corps and included a large part of the turret. Nowadays they tend to be Millennium Technology with nitrogen-filled lenses and cost about the same as a week in Benidorm.

Old Harry's mighty brass bottles hang on his chest like a Guardroom fire alarm. He has no hesitation in lending them.

'Here, try these then!' he'll challenge, clapping them to your brow with stunning force.

A stranger, peering into those murky caverns, may recoil with a cry of horror and disgust, as he sees what appears to be a host of huge tarantulas advancing along the coachroof in a blizzard. 'Back, back, you evil swine!' he may cry in distress, swiping out with his boots.

Old Harry soon rectifies this technical problem, restoring the delicate optical bloom to the lenses with his thumb inside the sleeve of his sweater.

'Now try THAT!' he invites. 'You won't find a glass like that on the market today.'

Well, you might, unless you were very, very cautious.

Charter or Martyr

On a charter holiday
Dad's a captain every day
But Mum despite her lowly status
Still makes him peel the goddam tatus.
'Oh shall we anchor for the night
In some foreign cove of rare delight?'
Says Mum 'I don't care where you park-it
So long as there's a supermarket.

It takes just one lousy summer and a holiday brochure through the letterbox at breakfast time to get mother going. 'I wonder why we can't have proper holidays like other people,' she asks the toast rack. Father, seeing all hope of a new cruising chute going down the spout, concentrates on the cornflake packet. He knows about *proper* holidays. Poolside sun loungers and clever dicks doing back flips... a coach trip to a carpet factory. He can't understand why she needs an all-over tan. Having spent the whole summer in wool and waterproofs, she now has a scarlet wind-blasted visage and a milk-white torso. Stripped, she looks like a toffee apple.

The fact that they did Start Point to The Needles in 12 hours, hosed along by a blast of wind and rain up the pushpit, evokes no joy. But he didn't get where he is today without learning a bit of diplomacy. Father books up for an end-of-season Special Package Mammoth Discounts charter holiday in the Med.

Instead of cooking, cleaning and throwing up in a temperature of 10°C, she can do it all at 35°C – in a wine-dark sea, air fares and starter-pack inclusive. It means a pre-dawn charter flight, following a vigil at Luton Airport with a taste in their mouths like chicken feathers and cough mixture. There is a choice of 'bareboat' charter, which means DIY skippering and an inventory that might suit a skull-and-candle hermit. It also includes polyprop berthing lines that untie themselves and a dodgy loo paper dispenser that delivers sheets in wads of ten at a time. Flotilla holidays we'll come to later.

Or you can go as 'paying crew'. This is like paying a drill sergeant to double you round the parade ground. Some return starry-eyed muttering Masefield while others, limping heavily, vow never even to look at another anchor rope or ride another turn. Unlike paying *guests*, paying crew do the washing up and have to sleep in their own wardrobes.

Guests arrive on Saturdays, two hours after the previous lot have limped ashore. The yacht owners, man and wife, having finished the cleaning, can enjoy the bliss of a thundering good row in private while keeping an eye on the town landing. It's like big game hunters staking out a water hole where a goat has been tethered. The skipper grabs the binos.

'This looks like them!' he grates. The mate wrests them from him. 'A pleated skirt and a knitted cardie!' she chokes brokenly. 'Oh, God, it's going to be one of those cruises!'

Novices with luggage, boarding a yacht for the first time, take up more room than a marching band. Getting them below is like watching potholers tackling a tricky sump. 'Mind your heads,' intones the mate.

'Clunk-owww!'

'Clunk-owww!'

'Clunk-ow!' comes the responses. It sounds like an ethnic xylophone.

'Well let's show you your bunks and locker space then,' says the mate resignedly, alert to the cries of incredulity to come. It's a hard way to earn a crust, running a PG boat. The first muster on deck to get under way sets the tone. The art is to let every-

body think they are helping, but without actually *doing* anything. Intent on the skipper's every word, they crowd around him, as though escorting a prisoner on remand.

A holiday in a PG boat means that the skipper decides where to go, a decision which is based upon wind direction, catching up on maintenance and pure sadism. 'So you want more sailing do you?' he chuckles evilly. 'Well, right then, *right!*' The mate exacts her own disciplines in harbour. The party changes its mind about dining ashore. They decide they'll stay aboard. Well they needn't expect any clever little sauces and *nouvelle cuisine*. It will be the *spécialité de maison* and lump it. Relations (like the cabbage) will be badly strained.

Bareboating for those with a little more experience can offer as many sour surprises as delights to the unwary. With Father in command, the odds are limitless. Having 'got his Yachtmaster', he will produce his certificate for all who wish to see it and a great many more who don't. It qualifies him to hold forth about anything and everything, from the Law of Storms to Greek Myths. 'Oh! you'll get no sharks here!' he laughs reassuringly. Then the waiter brings the bill.

The bareboater can either opt for the special rates levied for an early or late season booking, or go mid-season, in which case he can expect to be griddled pink and spend days huddled beneath a cockpit awning like a pixie under a toadstool. The late season charterer should take careful note of café sun awnings. Three rows of reef points plus rocks piled on the tables promises a spot of spirited sailing to come.

A further problem for the late-season charterer is that the maintenance gang, worn ragged by a season of unblocking loos and straightening stanchions, may have overlooked small deficiencies. Taps fall off like ripe plums, the galley pump has developed a second jet directed up the user's sleeve and Miriam has found 'a thing' in her locker. 'Let's have some air down here!' cries Father, tugging at a porthole. He stands holding it, examining it like some rare artefact.

There is really nothing to equal a flotilla holiday. End of statement. This means ten identical yachts crewed by parties all sharing an identical desire to hide a state of nautical virginity. The fleet is led by a nanny boat with a flotilla skipper, a hostess and a resident engineer on board.

Most, if not all, may be of Antipodean origin. The leader, a New Zealander, refers constantly and confusingly to 'litting go the inker'. The engineer in the standard uniform of vile shorts and grey singlet, has a string of letters after his name – mainly from HP firms and his wife's solicitors. One flick of his socket set and he can unbung a loo before it has had time to cool.

There is a daily briefing session over coffee when the flotilla skipper explains incomprehensible manoeuvres to uncomprehending skippers. They are reminded that they must not 'git ahid' of the leader boat and not to carry too much 'hidway' when 'littin' go inker'.

The programme consists of daysails in company and a 24-hour 'free' period when boats may roam at will, rendezvousing later. It is the equivalent of the package coach tour free halfday. The flotilla sailors end up in the same taverna, voted by all to be The Real Thing – a thatched lean-to with gritty octopus and a scratching dog.

Other highlights of the cruise include the beach barbecue – garlic bread and smoke through which shadowy figures grope and cough. There is also the 'fun dinghy race', not to be taken seriously, except by Father.

The only feature which may have marred this eventful cruise is the sanitary arrangements aboard boats which involve holding tanks. Just one extra night in harbour, plus the seafood platter all round, and you've got a bubbling breather-pipe about to go critical.

> *Oh we must go out to sea again*
> *Of that there is little doubt*
> *To be perfectly frank*
> *The holding tank*
> *Is in dire need of pumping out.*

The penultimate exercise is the Tidiest Boat Competition, a blatant con trick of such breathtaking gall that a time-share salesman would be left humble with admiration.

While the paid staff sit sipping cold beer in the local taverna, the *paying* crews, with the glittering prize of the Brillo Pad Trophy in mind, scrub, polish, coil and oil everything in sight.

Imagine hotels behaving that way. They'd have penalties for not cleaning up your own rubbish.

The communal supper marks the end of the cruise. There will be folk dancing. Father, primed high on ouzo, with trousers rolled up and a fair partner, prances under the laser eye of Lady-wife.

'Well you have to show a bit of willing, sweetie..' he oils later in self-defence. It seems he was showing more than willing. That little strumpet was young enough to have been his daughter and don't 'sweetie' me thank you very much.

Old Harry's appearance on the holiday cruising market was to 'break new ground' as they say in the chain gangs, and anybody hoping for deck games and dancing by moonlight was to be richly rewarded as they banged to windward in a force five.

'Go to sea as your forbears did!' invited his advertisement temptingly. It was an unspecific promise which might well have involved a Micke Finn down the old Ratcliff Highway and being dragged aboard a guano barque with their heels ploughing twin furrows across the quay.

'Learn the skills of the traditional sailor!' the ad continued, again unspecifically, and embracing such talents as chipping ballast and holy-stoning the deck. He offered hard work in the open air, healthy appetites and simple traditional fare – the formula for fitness in body and mind.

Gourmets would not be disappointed. Old Harry's speciality was a bouillabaisse of unique diversity, a biological quagmire of awesome maritime variety. 'Go on, spoil yourselves' he would invite, hinting at ruination on a massive scale. He stirred the pot. A pollock's head rose, took a look around as if on reconnaissance and, not liking what it saw, sank from view again.

Youth training proved more to his liking. A delegation of men from Social Services and the Probation Office, with leather patches on their sleeves and ginger moustaches, paid a preliminary visit. They found that CRL methods (clip-round-lughole) formed the basis of all training and that no expense had been spared in the provision of equipment for the young crew, namely a dozen new chipping hammers, a job lot of finger bandages, a bottle of Ellerman's Equine Rub and a sheep's head.

He guaranteed a regime designed to make men of them. Little old bent ones.

On the Trot

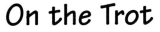

If you go down to the trots today
You may well find on occasion
The things you watches
Down open forehatches
Will further your education.

Apart from the acres of crimson flesh on Benidorm beach where Sybarites lie shoulder to shoulder anointing themselves with sand, crumbs and Nivea, you won't find a finer example of gross overcrowding than a visitor's berth in mid-August.

Lying on the trots – a description which implies a disregard for truth and an ill-advised extra helping of dodgy bouillabaisse – is not an experience one might recommend to either tyro or faint-hearted. 'Well we've got to go *somewhere*!' peeves father, motoring in circles. 'How about home?' murmurs Lady-wife without moving her lips, having just about had it up to here.

On either side of the trot rafts of homeless yachts clamp on alongside each other like some mammoth reptilian mating ritual in an ornamental pool. A scene of domestic activity is generated; an infant is hard at it untying and jettisoning other peoples' fenders. 'As long as he's busy bless him!' laughs a mum indulgently.

All day long crews clamber to and fro with eyes averted lest they glimpse something forbidden down forehatch or skylight. They skirt widely round cockpits as though to avoid something nasty on the pavement outside a pub.

Cockpits in such close proximity offer much the same social lottery as adjoining hospital beds where one becomes unwilling party to the groans, snorts and eructations of neighbours but lack the luxury of screens you can whip around.

The trots are where Father's best anecdote gets capped by the ungrateful swine he invited for drinks.

He gives his fond chuckle, the one which presages an anecdote the way slugs forecast rain. Unobserved, Lady-wife rolls her eyes.

'I remember a night off Alderney...' she mouths to herself.

'I remember a night off Alderney...' he trumpets. His humourless little tale drags to its totally flat dénouement. A brittle silence ensues.

'Hum,' says his guest hatefully. 'I well remember a night off Barbados...'

'I'll go and see if I can find some Twiglets,' says Lady-wife absenting herself, implying she has a full schedule of nest-building.

Blank hostility may greet latecomers to the trots, looking for someone to go alongside. It seems that one yacht is scheduled to leave at 4 am. Others are guarded by crew with fenders who crouch scowling, leaping to and fro in the Wimbledon shuffle. Alert eyes scan each arrival, hungry for a cockup. The neophyte skipper, innocent as Larry the Lamb, heads for his Nemesis. He is keen to follow correct nautical nomenclature. He clears his throat nervously.

'Ahoy!' he flutes.

'A *what*!' raps back the owner sharply, with hostility, turning his back.

Old Harry is as welcome as a song and dance routine at a funeral. He comes boiling down in his converted conger-clobberer, motor tyre fenders ready to print a town-and-country tread along virginal topsides. His great, rocking, single-pot enigne falls suddenly silent as he shorts it out with a spanner. It is a manoeuvre known as 'dropping down on the tide' – a descent heralded by a salvo of exploding plastic fenders.

Come nightfall a rare treat awaits the assembly. Old Harry hangs a reeking, oil lamp in his rigging where it belches clouds of rank and odorous black smoke. Smiling and with the air of a benefactor about to bestow a rare treat, he produces a concertina held together with more Sellotape than a charity parcel.

Spellbound listeners clap hands to ears and wince as he launches into his repertoire of hoots, groans and asthmatical wheezes. The concertina doesn't sound so good either. Nothing can interrupt his recital. 'Come on, let's have some requests!' he invites with the generosity that typifies the man.

'Oh for God's sake!' cry agonised listeners. It is a mistake.

Two Christmas carols and a requiem, accompanied by a thumping boot, are followed by *Abide with me*; not an invitation anybody felt inclined to accept.

Recyclists

Let's all have a dip in next-door's skip
While they're indoors watching the telly
Then like ghosts in the night
Vanish from sight
With an ironing board, two planks and a welly.

The Borough Council Recycling Officer mans a barricade of pram wheels and bedsprings. He is wearing a depressing pullover recycled from a disastrous knitted twinset ('sneer at winter's chills in this Quik-Knit skirt and jacket!'). It is like the defence of Rorke's Drift minus Zulus with assagais. 'Stand-to lads,' he tells his assistants, 'steady – here he comes!'

Old Harry's environmental contributions in terms of recycled junk are well known. Who gave us the electric earwig trap? Who introduced mud-surfing eh? Tell me that. In the sport's world his ballista shot-putter, contrived from TV ariel and gun-cotton, hit a new note – also the Town Hall clock. His hammer-thrower and caber-tosser, boons to contestants, rendered every sports stadium a hard hat area.

The urge to recycle has gripped the nation. Neighbours stand shoulder to shoulder poking empties into bottle banks, each eyeing the other's contribution – Special Offer Tesco Algerian versus Côte de Rhône at ten quid a bottle. An old lady, tea total from girlhood, but mucking out her attic lobs in a load of gin bottles. 'Who would have thought it, eh!'

bystanders hiss, 'her embroidering church hassocks and all!'

The wastepaper skip gags on its weekly feast of Sunday supplements. Father arrives with a bagful. 'Where am I supposed to stuff these then?' he asks huffily and rhetorically.

The householder unwise enough to hire a rubbish skip had better make up a flask of hot coffee and prepare for a long night's vigil. His task will be two-fold: keeping at bay stealthy neighbours with stained mattresses and shattered deckchairs, and thwarting the recyclers. Shadowy figures glide and whisper... 'Why look at this Cyril, nothing wrong with it!' Old Harry, a regular to such nocturnal assignations, staggers off well pleased with his haul. There will be one motor-mower less, but the world will profit from the first stern-wheeler paddle outboard.

'A crime to throw it out!' he chides hauling out an old TV screen. His forehatch is destined for a skylight and a trap for the unwary boot. The HM Customs Officer makes a snap visit. 'A quick trip below I think!' he tells his sidekick sternly and with uncanny precognition. He steps on it.

The dawn of the DIY era, Texas Homecare and enthusiasts emerging under sheets of hardboard on windy Saturday mornings with the great bounding strides of moon-walkers, gave fresh impetus to recycling.

There is surplus and *seemingly* surplus though. How many yachtsmen have rummaged under the settee mattresses in search of Admiralty chart 2693 *Approaches to Harwich*, in mounting panic and shoaling water not knowing that it has long since metamorphosised as a lampshade (Adult Education Beautify your home class)?

Take the Sunday joint. Like some ham actor making repeated and unrequested curtain calls to an audience interested only in forgetting the whole ghastly performance and going home, it appears and reappears throughout the week, cold with salad, in a goulash, minced and finally curried. The dog trots up the garden gingerly carrying a well-scraped bone.

Gaff rig, as is well known, fosters inventive recyclers the way broad beans attract thrip and Old Harry (whose all-terrain tyre fenders guarantee him an empty berth wherever he goes), scavenger of Green rubbish bins with their cornucopia of plastic bottles, is an inventive nutter of the first magnitude but rope is the problem. It is hard to find surplus rope.

The boom years for recyclers was the post-WW2 period when vast quantities of ex-naval and military equipment became available. Hammer-and-saw crackpots proliferated and a younger Old Harry blossomed like a conjurer's trick bouquet. Yachtsmen re-emerged to a world of peace warily, as if DIY neighbours had just stopped banging. It was the golden age of barmy entrepreneurs.

One might corner 100 crated engines and another, elsewhere, invest in 100 crated gearboxes. They searched dilligently to find one another like thwarted lovers, Kathy and Heathfield, hurtling together in head-on collision.

Old Harry speculated with forethought. He bought at bargain rates a job lot of Blanco and a gross of left-ankle khaki gaiters. Come WW3 he would need only to find a company of limping squaddies. His main investment proved less promising. The simultaneous purchase of a wooden hutted camp and a machine for making safety matches seemed to guarantee success. This was going to be big, as the man said triggering off the liferaft in the boot of his car.

Nowadays, like Tibetan fat-tailed sheep dragging their nourishment and wealth behind them on a small toboggan, yachties carry a fortune in designer clothing on their backs. Multi-hued Gortex breathables and puffers give them the unsettling appearance of Tellytubbies.

Post-war yachties had Milletts, a nationwide chain of retailers offering a bewildering selection of war-like garments for the impecunious but discerning yachtsman and woman at derisory cost. You could be kitted out in flying helmet, submariner's sweater, Eighth Army Shorts and Land Army wellies and over all the ubiquitous 'gas protection cape', vomit-coloured in a camouflage pattern and lending the wan-cheeked wearer the appearance of a mammoth frog, all for little over a fiver. You wouldn't find a better bargain in a long day's march. A long day's march might have been a better idea.

There was also a wide selection of instruments in little grey wooden boxes to be had, the functions of which were for the most part baffling. Others opened up new (and often totally unexpected) horizons for novice navigators. Yachties bent upon mastering the RAF bomber bubble-sextant drove shudderingly aground. Steering by ex-aircraft grid compass proved to be a new and exciting experience. 'Why, you can't go wrong!' rejoiced tyros, setting the grid on a 180° reciprocal.

77

Up Aloft with Old Harry

Old Harry, a regular customer of Messrs Milletts, where boots and waders of every type hung from the ceiling as if their wearers had suddenly mastered yogic flight, amassed bomb-sights, gas-boots, a machete and mule harness to be held pending some as yet undiscovered martime use. He also bought a pump.

Its original purpose long forgotten, the pump had the distinctive feature of being rotary and delivering a fat flow of liquid no matter in which direction the handle was turned. He at once installed it as a bilge pump, one pipe being immersed in the foul ordure of his bilge and the other overboard into the North Sea; a body of water not easily transferred from one place to another.

'Now then,' he invited, 'Watch the level lads!' He commenced cranking with vigour. The water level began to rise up his wellies. His smile began to erode at the corners. He cranked harder. The level rose higher.

'Help, help I'm sinking!' he howled.

And he was. And he did.

Glossary of nautical terms

(selected to enrich the vocabulary of the novice)

A

ABAFT	I have had a bath
AHEAD	A marine toilet
AHEAD (Full)	Quick go get a plumber
ALOFT	Place to store garden furniture in winter
A'LOW	A greeting, eg A'low sailor
ALONGSIDE	Also a short side, eg the stern Taking stern measures
ANCHOR	A form of battering ram used when berthing during Cowes Week
ANCHORING	A craving for something
ANEMOMETER	A 'timing' instrument, eg 'any-moment-a' gale will, etc...
ANTIFOUL	Table manners of visiting relative
ASTERN GEAR	Sombre garments worn by High Court Judge

B

BACKWASH	A loofah sponge
BAGGYWRINKLES	Unsuccessful face-lift
BARQUE	Worse than a bight
BECALM	Common nautical order. 'For heaven's sake, Rodney, stop flapping!'
BITT A CABLE	Not much cable
BITTER END	A bite on the bottom
BLEEDING (diesel engine)	We need a bleeding engineer, mate
BODY PLAN	Self-measurement diagram in mail-order catalogue
BOOM CRUTCH	A painful injury
BOOT TOPPING	A welly full of water
BOTTLESCREW	Prison warder who sells booze on the side
BOW (also BOW-WOW!)	Cry from forr'd as about to hit quayside
BOW FENDER	At both ends
BOWLINE (also ten-pin)	Game once played on Plymouth Hoe
BRING UP	You'll feel a whole lot better
BUBBLE SEXTANT	My sextant has fallen overboard
BUOYANCY TANK	An amphibious military vehicle
BUNK	Total rubbish
BURGEE	Golfing term, eg 'There's this for a burgee.'
BUTTOCK LINE	See BODY PLAN

C

CABIN SOLE	A fish dish. Scraped up off the, etc
CAPSIZE	Size of hat. If too large pack sweatband with newspaper

CHAIN LOCKER	A padlock
CHART DRAWER	A naval cartographer
CLOVE HITCH	Painful skin allergy to cloves
COCKED HAT	A courteous gesture
COMPANION(WAY)	Superior domestic employee in lisle stockings
COMPASS ROSE	A lady of easy virtue
COPPER FASTENED	Handcuffed
CROSS BEARING	A religious procession
CUDDY	Yes, he could
CURRENT INSET	Railway buffet bun

Copper fastened

D

DEADLIGHTS	Offal, eg chitterlings, tripe, etc
DEAD BEAT	A funeral march
DEADEYE	A glass eye
DEADWOOD	Rotten
DIPPING LUG	A lowering of the head
DOG WATCH	A day at the greyhounds
DOUBLING (the angle on the bow)	Usually due to faulty astern gear
DOUBLENDER	An overdraft

BUN

Current inset

E

ECHO SOUNDING	Typically, Yooo-hooo
EYE SPLICE	Cockney dialect, eg the freezer or ice plice

F

FAIRWAY	Quite a distance
FENDER (A)	One who commits an offence
FIN KEEL	Narrow keel. Not very fick
FISHERMAN'S BEND	An occupational ailment
FLASHING BUOY	Typically wears long grey raincoat
FO'C'S'LE	Some folks will, some won't
FOOT LOCKER	Manacles
FOUL HAWSE	An objectionable animal
FOUNDER (I've)	Bibulous cry. In a marina. Returned revellers find yacht
FOUR POINT FIX	Toasting fork
FUTTOCKS	An expletive

Fisherman's Bend

G

GALLEY DRAWER	A stowage for dead torch batteries, corks, etc
GEARBOX	A suitcase
GETTING UNDER WEIGH	A shopkeeper's con. An unseen finger placed on scales
GIMBALLS	Figure it out for yourself
GO ABOUT	Boxing term, eg go a bout with Joe Bugner, etc
GOOSENECK	A kiss on the neck
GRANNY KNOT	Grandma is not included
GREAT CIRCLE	Pedestrian movement when encountering flag-seller
GROUND TACKLE	Goalkeeper's technique
GUDGEON AND PINTLE	A firm of family solicitors

H

HALF MASTED	Result of low bridge
HANGING KNEES	Distressing condition. Never wear tights
HANDY BILLY	A notorious pickpocket
HEAVE TO	Cornish dialect, eg 'he has two'
HIGH AND DRY	Drunk and still thirsty
HORIZONTAL PARALLAX	Drunker still
HURRICANE	A high speed walking stick

I

INSET AND OUTSET	A dentist's instructions to patient
INBOARD	All meals included
ISOBAR	An iced lolly
INTERNATIONAL CODE	Widespread flu epidemic

J

JACKSTAY	Approx nine months before Jill's day
JETTY	The Abominable Snowman
JOLLY ROGER	Will never be invited to another dinner in *my* house
JURY RIGGED	A form of bribery
JUMPER STRUT	Distinctive walk of man in new jumper when wife watching

K

KATABATIC	A cat catching mice in the loft
KEDGE	A fish dish
KNEES (Hanging)	A sign of old age

L

LANDFALL	An avalanche
LEEWAY	A Chinese philosopher
LONE YACHTSMAN	Yachtsman with marine mortgage
LLOYD'S SURVEY	A sort of lookout
LONG SPLICE	The place where Mr and Mrs Long live
LOOKOUT	I have just dropped a hammer
LOW PRESSURE	Fetch a plumber
LUNAR CYCLE	A vehicle developed under the space programme.

M

MARLINE SPIKE	The dreadful young couple next door
MANILA	The man is getting worse
MAXIMUM DRAFT	The table nearest the entrance
MIDSHIPMAN	Confined to the middle of the boat
MOORING PILES	Painful occupational ailment afflicting foredeck crew
MUDBANK	A repository for mud. A doormat

N

NAVAL PIPE	The umbilical cord
NET TONNAGE	The weight of a net
NIGHT PASSAGE	Leads to bathroom. Favourite bed for black labradors
NIGHT WATCH	Has luminous dial and alarm function
NUN BUOY	A nun's son

O

ON THE TROTS	Unfortunate bowel condition following package holiday
OILSKIN	Suntan lotion
OUTBOARD	Lodging allowance
OVERLAP	Position of secretary seeking promotion
OVERALL LENGTH	The length of an apron

Pan Pan

P

PAN PAN	Emergency call heard in hospital wards
PICK-UP LINE	A kerb-crawler's technique
PLIMSOLL LINE	Muddy footprints
PLUMMER BLOCK	Usually a toothpaste tube cap or-you-know, calling for plumber
POOPED	Should have gone easy on the duty free
PORT HOLE	A bodega or drinking den
PROPELLER CREEP	Contemptuous term for one who motors all the time
PULPIT	To mash something

Q

QUARTER BERTH	Only one quarter available for sleeping
QUICK FLASH	A punishable offence

R

RELATIONSHIP	Manned by relations who are beginning to get up my nose, etc
RIDING TURN	An equestrian circus act
RIDING TURN	It is my turn for a ride
RIGHT-HAND LAY	My/your side of the bed
RIDING LIGHT	No cargo
RISE-AND-FALL	Attempted curtsey on polished parquet
ROUND TURN AND TWO HALF HITCHES	A sort of sailor's hornpipe
ROLLING HITCH	A drunken sailor's hornpipe
RUNNING OUT A KEDGE	Stock of kedge almost exhausted

S

SAGGING	In need of a face-lift
SAMSON POST	Samuel is sitting on a post
SEACOCK	Mate of sea hen
SEMAPHORE	And sem are against
SHACKLE PIN	Found in scuppers and unidentifiable
SHEET ANCHOR	Method of hanging on to your side in double bed
SKIN FITTING	A body stocking
SPUNYARN	Told some real porkies
STERN WHEELER	A grumpy cyclist
STORM CONE	A harbinger of bad weather. Caused by tight-fitting shoe
STRUM BOX	A banjo
SWINGING ROOM	A disco

T

TARPAULIN	Thanks, Pauline
TOE STRAP	A device for trapping toes
TOPPING LIFT	Expression of gratitude by hitch-hiker
TRIPPING LINE	eg tent guy rope
TRIMMING (Sails)	Trim your jib (cut off its sticky-out bits)
TYPHOON	A brand of tea

U

UP-AND-DOWN (the anchor)	Can't the skipper make up his mind
UNDER CANVAS	Camping out
UPSETTING MOMENT	eg when father tipped the Admiral to find him a taxi

V

VERY LIGHT	Not heavy
VHF RADIO	Very Height of Fatuity, eg inter-yacht traffic
VISITORS' BUOYS	Little swine in baseball caps driving high speed dories

W

WARNING LIGHT	Seen in wife's eye when hitting the club claret
WAKE	An Irish funeral
WEATHER HELM	An optional extra when buying at Boat Show
WHIPPING	Forbidden under EU rules
WITHEY	Cornish dialect, 'Is he with ee?'
WINTER COVER	A canvas chute for deluging owner

X
XEBEC

All right, *you* think of something, cleverdick

Y
YAWL

South Carolina accent for 'You-all' (*Gone with Wind*, etc)

Z
ZINC ANODE

I zinc I knowed the answer to this one